fresh ink
Published Writings

CHLOE LIZOTTE

Copyright © 2011 by Chloe Lizotte

All rights reserved. No part of this book may be reproduced
or transmitted in any form or by any means, electronic or mechanical,
including photocopying, recording, or by any other information
storage and retrieval system, without the written permission
of the author, except where permitted by law.

ISBN: 978-0-9847185-0-4

Printed in the United States of America

emerson books

Published by emerson books
Concord, MA • www.thoughtleading.com

October 2011

For Pop and his daily words of wisdom
"Die methode ist alles"

table of contents

BEGINNING
Ready to Start: A Personal Narrative 1

ECCENTRICS
Bronson Alcott: An Educator Apart from the Rest 9
John Brown: Conductor of Resistance 13
Thomas Carlyle: Bizarre but Appreciated 17
William Ellery Channing: A Poet Misunderstood 21
Margaret Fuller: "I Accept the Universe!" 25
William James: Depression, Boredom, Hidden Talents 29
Henry Wadsworth Longfellow: Glass Half-Full 33
James Gamble Rogers: Conventionally Unconventional 37
Elizabeth Cady Stanton: Her Iron Will Opened Doors 41
Mark Twain: Not Necessarily Safe to Travel 45
Francis Wayland: Wise, Unconventional, and Majestic 49

ARTS/ENTERTAINMENT
Black Swan: Film Review 55
Boats Against the Current: The Role of the Green Light
in *The Great Gatsby* 59
Harry Potter and the Deathly Hallows – Part I: Film Review 63
Ignore the Ignorant by The Cribs: CD Review 67
Life Without Michael: Reflections on "The Office" in Transition . . . 71
Life in Transition: Holden Caulfield's Journey into Adulthood 77

ARTS/ENTERTAINMENT (continued)

Krakauer on McCandless: Into the Enigma 83
Oscars 2011 89
Radiohead: *The King of Limbs* and Future Branches 95
The Resistance by Muse: CD Review 99
Santiago as the Hemingway Code Hero:
A Study in Grace Under Pressure 103
The Suburbs by Arcade Fire: CD Review 107
Shine a Light: Alfred Hitchcock's Usage of Lighting in Film 111

HISTORY and POLITICAL AFFAIRS

Demystifying a Legend: Reviewing Stacy Schiff's *Cleopatra* 117
England Faces Aftermath of Violent Riots 125
How the Youth Culture of the 1920s Reinvigorated America 129
Idi Amin and the Tanzanian Invasion of Uganda –
Research Memo 137
Letter from Birmingham Jail:
Constructing the Optimal Argument 141

MISCELLANEOUS

A Tale of Montreal 149
Competing with the System Itself: A Speech 153
Unique at All Costs: An Editorial 159
Thoreau Challenge 163

Acknowledgements 173
About the Author 175

about the book

All articles and essays in this book have been previously reviewed by an editor at a respected newspaper, journal, or website and selected for publication. No chapter content has been included that has not fulfilled that requirement.

The essays in this book reflect where I've been, what I've seen, how I've reacted, and what I've concluded. They speak well to my journey up to this stage in my life.

BEGINNING

Ready to Start: A Personal Narrative

Published by Teen Ink

"I thought the goal of making a record was to document something worth remembering. So why name your album something as boring as *The Suburbs*?" I looked up from my issue of Q Magazine to stare blankly at the plane seat in front of me as I pondered this question. Realizing that the seat would not have anything constructive to say about this sort of topic, I quickly averted my gaze to the window. The fields of the English countryside whizzed past in a torrent of green and brown as the plane began its descent. I simultaneously shoved the magazine into my backpack and the issue out of my mind, ready to enjoy a few weeks' break from the monotony of my hometown. A vacation in a city like London, no less! With its incredible alternative scene, London represented a safe haven for those invested in listening to top-notch music. Being a person who refers to members of rock bands by their first names as if they are close family friends, visiting a city like London meant returning to my long-lost hometown.

The Suburbs. Nothing about the name stimulated me, yet the Canadian indie rock juggernaut that is Arcade Fire had released its third full-length record to the world under this dull moniker. For a title so seemingly forgettable, the album proved inescapable during my week in London. Stacks of music magazines at a convenience store would be emblazoned with Arcade Fire cover stories. A simple tube trip meant passing at least three posters displaying the cover art. Even billboards would feature that image of a car parked in front of a nondescript brick house, the words "Arcade Fire presents *The Suburbs*" bold amidst the muted neutrals. Those familiar with the indie rock scene will not be surprised by this amount of publicity – the fact that Arcade Fire is so well-respected by fans and critics alike made the release of this album An Extremely Big Deal. Familiar as I was, I still firmly believed that substituting the word "Annoying" for "Big" would be more apt. I checked the view from my hotel window every morning to confirm that Big Ben was, indeed, still standing, and had not transformed itself into that commonplace brick house overnight.

Heathrow Airport was, so to speak, the straw that broke the camel's back. On the way to catch our flight to Paris, I blinked emotionlessly for a few seconds when I encountered the airport's CD shop. Five full rows of that car and that house, cloned and ready for consumption, taunted me upon entering. The fight-or-flight mechanism kicked in, and I marched straight into the flames, snatching a copy from the top row. I vaguely heard the cashier complimenting me on my taste in music after I slammed the CD down on the front desk. I suppose I had to crack a smile after the textbook example of colloquial English dialect, "Brilliant album! Only ten quid, too."

Paris gave me my first opportunity to experience the record. Waiting for the rest of my family to embark on a day of touring, I slouched somewhat comfortably in a wire chair in the hotel lobby. It was the sort of chair that had been added as an afterthought, as if the interior designers had said to themselves, "Maybe someone would want to sit here! In the *lobby*! Fancy that! Probably a rare occurrence, though, so let's go bargain hunting at Ikea." I chuckled to myself at the thought, momentarily curbing my boredom. The monotony of the pouring rain diverted my attention, creating a violent din as the water fell relentlessly on the stones in the hotel courtyard. I wasn't even able to observe the behavior of individual droplets – it was the type of rain that formed a wall, barricading feeble humans from the outside world. Slightly intimidated by such a personification, I fumbled around my pockets for my iPod to block out the noise.

Scrolling through the albums, those familiar two words appeared in Arial font. *The Suburbs.* Why not. My thumb made contact with the words.

The first chord swept me away into the tide. Lilting piano chords with bass and a straight drumbeat flowed effortlessly through my headphones in a progression that naturally complemented the rain outside. The water took form, droplets falling onto the trees in patterns that could only make sense in conjunction with this particular soundscape. Such a simple four-chord melody, yet so effortlessly stunning. An unknown memory rather than a revelation.

Vocals soon cascaded into the mix, a new instrument as opposed to a necessary ingredient for an accessible record. *In the suburbs I, I learned to drive...*

The glass door separating me from the falling rain soon became the windshield of that familiar car, wheels turning, landscape blurring, rain drumming in 4/4 time to the rhythm. *Sometimes I can't believe it, I'm moving past the feeling.*

The words evoked vivid memories - all those hours scrawling hurried journal entries to myself, small aphorisms to document my thought processes as a high school sophomore. *The present is transitory*, I had written time and time again. *We don't live in the moment, but rather move past the blurred collection. Movement...*

High school limbo seemed tolerable when taking this into account. The constraint of walking the halls. Not that I wasn't socially accepted – I had found a group of people I enjoyed – but isolation often overwhelmed me. Respected and acknowledged, yet far from understood.

April. Soggy mid-afternoon. "Northeastern," my friend Ashley had declared when the topic of conversation rolled around to colleges. "That's where I want to go."

"No hesitation there!" I quipped in return.

"Well, it's perfect, isn't it?" She paused to collect her thoughts. "My sister goes there and it's close to home." Another pause. "Where else would I go?"

"I dunno...elsewhere?"

That word proved incredibly puzzling. *"Elsewhere?"* Ashley tasted the word and wanted to spit it out, a grimace reflecting her thoughts.

I chuckled. "You know, maybe somewhere out of state? It'll be your chance to see the world *beyond* Concord and Boston. Think about it – you could go anywhere!" My eyes widened as I saw the horizon stretching out in front of me, airplanes taking off and landing somewhere exotic. "You know....the world of *not Massachusetts.*"

Ashley's head tilted to a 45-degree angle. Squinted eyes indicated I hadn't quite broken through.

"Well, I dunno, maybe it's just me then," I quickly backtracked. *It can't just be me, can it?* "I mean, Boston's great, I like it here."

"Yeah! Exactly! Why leave when everything's so great here?" Ashley's usual smile returned as she considered everything she loved about the Boston area.

"Right, right," I agreed half-heartedly.

Now I'm ready to start, you're not sure. The album drifted onwards, the lyrics quickly becoming the perceptive friend I never had. *Now you're knocking at my door saying: "Please come out with us tonight." But I would rather be alone than pretend I feel all right.*

A cold shudder of recognition shifted me in my suddenly uncomfortable chair. I thought I had erased all those memories in the aftermath. Then again, when a portable disaster of a social life shapes someone's freshman year of high school, nothing is entirely forgotten. Blurred, patchy snapshots popped and fizzed in my head, not quite taking any linear form. Surrounded by people, but always alone. Gradually becoming aware that my life was taking a different path than those of my friends. Steadily becoming unable to recognize my real friends. Lack of communication. Lack of enjoyment spending time together. *Friends don't ignore each other quite like this, do they?* Leaving the lunch table in a haze of fury and confusion. Earphones in, world out.

"My friends dropped me in high school" is likely one of the most prevalent clichés one can ever encounter, but this doesn't lessen the impact of the emotions involved. I couldn't face the memories again – I've never been one to dwell extensively on the past. Always focusing on the future. Everything else is transport. Besides, my story had a happy ending. Sophomore year ushered new people into my life – uncomplicated, easygoing friendships. A refreshing change from what I was used to. A smile crept across my face when I remembered a few inside jokes of ours, tapping my foot as my attention drifted back to *The Suburbs*. I fell into a musical trance as the record progressed, curling up inside these sound waves that understood me so well.

Rhythmic acoustic guitar chords opened "Wasted Hours," the eleventh track on the album. A shot of adrenaline rushed through me as I realized this number was in the double digits. Had ten songs finished already? Paying attention to running time seemed irrelevant - the album progressed as one musical thought with many movements instead of a collection of sixteen songs. The guitar lulled me back into my trance as the rain continued out the window. *Wishing you were anywhere but here, you watch the life you're living disappear. And now I see, we're still kids in buses longing to be free.*

I began to nod my agreement, easily identifying with the notion. Mature enough to feel trapped by the stagnant nature of life in the sleepy suburbs, but still too young to break out and see the world. Wanting more from a monotonous cycle of life – wake up, eat, go to school, go home, do homework, eat again, do more homework, sleep, repeat – but unable to actually do anything that might change the system. I finally understood that I *wasn't* alone in feeling this way. This record filled a void. Rather than feeding teenage angst, they symbolized movement, even hope. Beyond my small town, my suburban prison, people like me actually *existed*. My desperation to escape the constraints of the suburbs was no longer uniquely my own struggle.

Waiting out the time is easier said than done, but soon enough, this limbo would be a trivial memory. "The transitory present," I reminded myself out loud. There was too much to look forward to beyond the borders of the suburbs. The future, the unknown, the *not Massachusetts* all lay before me.

Here, in my place and time, and here in my own skin, I can finally begin.

ECCENTRICS

Bronson Alcott: An Educator Apart from the Rest

Published in The Concord Journal

Perhaps the most education-oriented transcendentalist in the movement's heyday was Louisa May Alcott's father, Amos Bronson. This turned out to be quite ironic given that the Alcott family's patriarch himself experienced almost no formal education as a child. Later to become renowned for his boundless determination, a young Bronson was able to teach himself to read and write merely by scrawling letters on the floorboards of his kitchen with charcoal. Then, as a teenager, Bronson traveled to the southern United States as a solicitor of books and various goods, intent on earning some money for his destitute family. This action plan however left Bronson in significant debt despite exposing him to an upper class Southern lifestyle that he had never seen in his native Connecticut. Perhaps influenced by this exposure, upon returning to New England, he elected to switch careers and pursue a job in education.

Bronson worked in various schools for about ten years before he opened the Temple School in Boston in 1834. His progressive and radical approach quickly set him apart from other schoolteachers of his day. Bronson considered it his job not to merely dictate facts to the children but to guide them as they discovered and developed their own abilities. Students were encouraged to be inquisitive and open-minded in class, and Bronson attempted to expose them to art, music, and nature, subjects which were rarely mentioned in other schools. Furthermore, Bronson was famously opposed to corporal punishment. Rather than striking the children when they were disobedient, he would reverse the roles and ask students to strike his own hand – if the students were not paying attention, Bronson assumed that this was his own fault. Despite the innovation of Bronson's teaching, his ideas perplexed the public. Many parents pulled their children out of his school, and the Temple School was closed after a mere five years.

A true transcendentalist, Bronson quickly became friends with Ralph Waldo Emerson, Margaret Fuller, Nathaniel Hawthorne, Elizabeth Palmer Peabody and Henry David Thoreau, among others. He wrote a number of books as well as a column in the Concord-based transcendentalist publication *The Dial*, featuring his "Orphic Sayings" – bizarre, enigmatic, philosophical statements which unfortunately often only confused readers instead of enlightening them. But his friends had great faith in him, particularly Emerson who pushed the Concord school board to appoint Bronson its first superintendent, a position he enthusiastically accepted despite a miniscule salary. Needless to say, he completely reinvented the Concord school system's curriculum, something which the town welcomed.

1879 saw the opening of Bronson's School of Philosophy where he held various lectures for adults, quite possibly the first adult education center in America. In stark contrast to the Temple School he opened forty years earlier, the press greeted the School of Philosophy with glowing reviews. His star was finally on a rise, a testament to his lifelong dedication to well-meaning unorthodox ideas.

John Brown: Conductor of Resistance

Published in The Concord Journal

One of the defining figures of the pre-Civil War era, John Brown stood firm in his beliefs and fought for equality in the face of violent opposition. Born in 1800 to a Calvinist household, Brown was exposed to his father's anti-slavery beliefs from an early age. His father often stated that slavery was fundamentally wrong in the eyes of God. In addition, Brown's earliest childhood memories helped form the groundwork for his future. At age 12, while traveling through Michigan to deliver cattle, he witnessed a man viciously beat his boy slave. This moment never left him.

Brown cycled through various professions over the course of his life. Though he originally wanted to become a Congregationalist minister in Massachusetts, he was forced to return home to Ohio due to an eye disorder. He then cycled through various professions over the course of his life – running a tannery, selling wool, breeding farm animals. However, most of his business ventures failed as his heightened idealism led him to trust manipulative and unscrupulous manufacturers, proving much less discerning than the average businessman.

He eventually filed for bankruptcy and shifted his focus to human struggle and suffering. After the 1837 murder of Elijah P. Lovejoy, a major abolitionist, at the hands of a pro-slavery mob, Brown publicly declared that he would dedicate his life to the abolitionist movement, a statement which far understated the true meaning of his words.

In the hope that he could function as a "kind father" to escaped slaves, for example, Brown carried out his duties as a "conductor" on the Underground Railroad by housing fugitives. However, Brown is far more renowned for his militant actions in the anti-slavery movement. He confided to Frederick Douglass in 1847 that he felt he needed to begin a war in order to end slavery, going so far as to claim that God had directly commissioned him to lead slave revolts. The famous Bleeding Kansas, a string of violent anti-slavery events in the 1850s, saw John Brown at the forefront of many bloody rebellions.

Afterwards, traveling through the Northeast under the alias Nelson Hawkins, he gathered troops and funds for an attack on Virginia, one of the most pro-slavery states in the union at that time. Six prominent abolitionists, including William Lloyd Garrison, Theodore Parker and Frank Sanborn, became enthusiastic benefactors, known collectively as the Secret Six.

Brown's most famous scheme added significantly to building antebellum tension – his raid on Virginia's Harpers Ferry Armory in 1859. Brown wanted to arm the slaves of the surrounding area so they could defend themselves while they escaped their plantations and fled the state. Though his plan appeared fairly successful at first, as he was easily able to infiltrate the armory, Colonel Robert E. Lee soon led the state militia into the town and captured Brown. He was then tried and hanged for treason soon after, but became a martyr after his death to his sympathizers in the North. One of them, Henry David Thoreau, memorialized him with these words:

"He did not recognize unjust human laws, but resisted them as he was bid…No man in America has ever stood up so persistently and effectively for the dignity of human nature."

Thomas Carlyle: Bizarre But Appreciated

Published in The Concord Journal

Scottish-born philosopher-writer Thomas Carlyle ended up taking a radically different turn in life than the one he had originally anticipated. Born in 1795 to a Calvinist household in southern Scotland, Carlyle initially assumed he would become a priest. However, he came to question his faith in such a way that his changing belief system led him away from what his church had to offer. In fact, Carlyle's very ability to question ultimately brought him great recognition as a philosopher even if his writing is the main reason he is now remembered.

Carlyle's major work, *Sartor Resartus* – Latin for "The Tailor Re-tailored" – introduced a unique style of writing, later dubbed "Carlylese." This writing style would often combine a mixture of both German and English words, sometimes altering the word order of a sentence by effectively writing sentences backwards. In addition, *Sartor Resartus* was a highly complex work on its own, mixing fact with fiction while weaving a story that indirectly commented on Carlyle's philosophy. Needless to say, the public found the book both bizarre and unreadable, making it difficult for Carlyle to get it published. Still, those who were able to appreciate Carlyle's eccentric style, including Ralph Waldo Emerson in the 19th Century and Dwight Eisenhower a century later, greatly admired the Scottish writer.

While Carlyle is well known for his interest in philosophy, it was his interest in history that paved the way for even more literature. After moving from Scotland to London in 1834, he started work on an extensive two-volume recollection of the French Revolution, fittingly titled *The French*

Revolution, A History. After completing the first draft of the first volume, Carlyle lent it to his friend philosopher John Stuart Mill to read. Murphy's Law struck unexpectedly when Mill's maid mistook the manuscript for waste paper and threw the only draft of Carlyle's intensive history into the fireplace to burn. Surprisingly, Carlyle showed very little anger, and simply started from scratch to rewrite the entire first volume once again. *The French Revolution* was finally published in 1837.

As Carlyle grew older, he became more and more convinced that fascism was the ideal form of government. His writing began to reflect this sentiment, causing his interests to move away from his earlier existential musings. Passing at the age of 85 in London, Thomas Carlyle is thus destined to be forever remembered as "that eccentric Scottish writer" who raised many eyebrows during England's otherwise exceedingly straight-laced Victorian era.

William Ellery Channing: A Poet Misunderstood

Published in The Concord Journal

The life and career of the poet William Ellery Channing defied and rejected many of the social standards of his time. Ellery's life began in 1817 in Boston, Massachusetts, sharing his name with his great-grandfather, who signed the Declaration of Independence, as well as with his uncle, a Unitarian minister. Growing up, the younger William Ellery had quite a rebellious streak and was even expelled from Harvard University in 1834 before the end of his freshman year! This did not bother young Ellery, though – he quickly discovered that he preferred spending time on more free-form activities rather than the denser subjects he had been studying at Harvard. Just a year later in fact, he had already began to publish quirky essays under a pen name, an exercise that made it clear to Ellery what his true calling was– to become a poet.

Shortly after this revelation, Ellery decided to relocate to rural Illinois. While there, he constructed a floorless log cabin where he could farm and live in isolation from the public. However, after only a year, he moved to the metropolis of Cincinnati where some of his extended family resided. In this more energetic environment, Ellery resumed writing poetry. Much of his material in those days was inspired by Ralph Waldo Emerson's essay *Nature*, which explains why Ellery chose to send his poetry to be published in the transcendentalist journal *The Dial*, of which Emerson was a member of the staff. At that point, Margaret Fuller was the editor of The Dial, an extraordinary coincidence in that Ellery, around that same time, happened to meet Margaret's younger sister, Ellen, in Cincinnati. The two married a year after meeting and left Cincinnati to live in Concord, Massachusetts, the home base of *The Dial*.

Ellery's poetry, however, was not particularly popular, such that he could only survive financially from donations from family and friends. In fact, he was more often criticized than praised for his work, his poems striking many as quite abstract as well as progressive in terms of transcendentalist thinking, concepts that tended to lead his readers astray. One of his more well-known critics was Edgar Allen Poe, commenting that "it may be said in [Ellery's] favor that nobody ever heard of him." However, Emerson praised the beauty of Ellery's writings, and continued to publish his transcendentalist philosophizing in *The Dial*.

Ellery generally disliked the limits society placed on him, preferring to live in seclusion from others. Decidedly eccentric and inclined to wander rather than to stay still, his wife chose to leave him in 1853 as he continued to be incapable of providing any sort of security or income for her or their four children. Despite his shortcomings as a husband, however, his personality made him a worthy companion of Concord's most famous eccentric Henry David Thoreau. For a time, the two were practically inseparable. In fact, it was Ellery who first suggested that Thoreau experiment with a hermit lifestyle by building a cabin at Walden Pond. Their remarkable friendship led Ellery to become the first biographer of Thoreau, writing *Thoreau, the Poet-Naturalist* in 1873.

Ellery passed away two days before Christmas in 1901 and was buried in Sleepy Hollow Cemetery in Concord. Fittingly enough, his grave is directly across from that of Thoreau on Author's Ridge. Emerson once noted, "In walking with Ellery you shall always see what was never before shown to the eye of man." Though misunderstood by many, Ellery's legacy exists for those who revel in the magic of nature as the same way that he did and who seek a refreshing perspective on the natural world.

Margaret Fuller: "I Accept the Universe!"

Published in The Concord Journal

Margaret Fuller met Ralph Waldo Emerson in the summer of 1836 just before transcendentalism began, when Emerson was finishing writing "Nature." At first, Emerson was unimpressed with her. He thought Margaret very "plain" and found himself distracted by her "nasal voice." Yet Margaret eventually won him over such that Waldo grew to appreciate her level of intellect and her personality. "I remember that she made me laugh more than I liked," he later said, "for I was, at that time, an eager scholar of ethics, and had tasted the sweets of solitude and stoicism, and so I found something profane in the hours of amusing gossip into which she drew me."

Before meeting Emerson, Margaret had attended several schools where she learned German and Italian. But before long she decided she was unchallenged by other people she knew, viewing most women as beneath her level intellectually. Because of this, Margaret came to be thought of as quite vain. At one point, she proclaimed "I accept the universe!" as if the universe should feel like it had earned her respect. She also once announced one day that she had "never met her intellectual equal."

In 1839, Margaret began to sponsor a series of seminars for women called "Conversations." She invited women from areas around Boston, from wives of famous intellectuals to women working on starting up their own careers, oftentimes as writers. The women debated many subjects, including mythology, art, education, and women's rights. The many resulting discussions inspired provided Margaret's cardinal work, *Woman in the*

Nineteenth Century. Written in 1845, her book is still considered a classic piece of feminist writing today.

In 1840, Margaret became the first editor of transcendentalist magazine The Dial. She spent much time in Concord attempting to persuade less-than-eager writers to write for the publication. But upon reading what was submitted, she frequently became disgusted, rejecting the material outright and replacing it with her own essays. Consequently for about two years, she wrote the lion's share of each issue herself. Emerson then took over as editor, although sources say Margaret actually continued to do most of actual editing. In 1843, Margaret contributed to The Dial a clarion call for women's equality titled "The Great Lawsuit: Man vs. Men and Woman vs. Women."

In 1844, Horace Greeley asked Margaret to become book review editor for the New York Tribune. Margaret accepted and became very successful in this position. She began writing reviews not only on books but on New York art and culture as well.

In May of 1850, after three years of living in Italy with a man 10 years younger than she (records are unclear if they actually married) and their young son, Margaret and her family boarded a ship to America. Tragedy however struck when the ship's captain died of smallpox and his less experienced replacement crashed the ship into a sandbar within sight of Fire Island, NY. The powerful current claimed the lives of Margaret and her family and other passengers. Henry David Thoreau was sent to search the wreckage for her remains but none were found. A manuscript she had been working on about the Italian revolution was lost forever as well.

For the 40 years Margaret Fuller was alive, she did her best to make a difference in the world, and it worked. Was she a true eccentric or merely a fierce pioneer dedicated to the principle of equal rights? Whatever the case, her work as a transcendentalist and a feminist certainly propelled the state of American culture miles forward, one of many reasons Emerson had been happy to know her. No less than Susan B. Anthony and Elizabeth Cady Stanton wrote that Margaret "possessed more influence on the thought of American women than any woman previous to her time." I'm sure if Margaret were alive today she'd be pleased to see that many of her dreams of gender-equality have finally come true, although she'd most likely also feel we've still got a way yet to go.

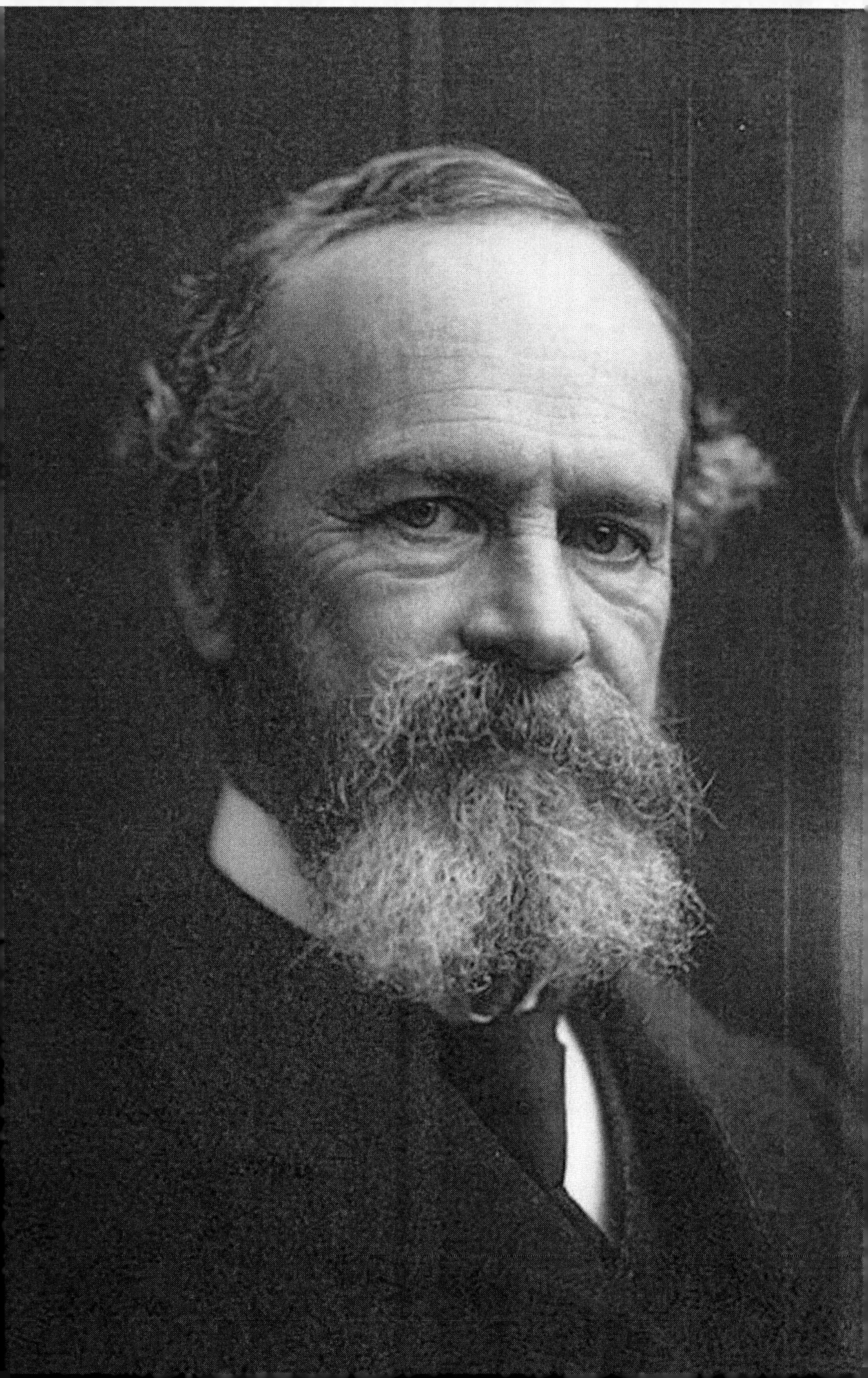

William James: Depression, Boredom, Hidden Talents

Published in The Concord Journal

Born in Manhattan in 1842, William James's life followed a meandering road full of unexpected forks before he discovered what he truly enjoyed. In his eccentric father's quest to ensure that his children received an unparalleled education, William's family had relocated transatlantic four times before he turned 18. Henry James Sr. chose to move whenever he noticed William gravitating towards indulging his interest in the arts such as when, as a teenager, William became enamored with the idea of becoming a painter. This aspiration did not fit in with Henry Sr.'s vision of William's future, in a realm such as science or philosophy. So, frequent changes of continent characterized the driven Henry's attempt to divert his son's attention from artistic pursuits.

Ultimately, to Henry's delight, William chose science upon enrolling at Harvard. However, William soon found himself bored with these studies so that, after a few years, he moved on to Harvard Medical School, thinking medicine would be better able to sustain his monetary needs for the future. Still uninspired after a year studying medicine, William chose to accompany world-class geologist Louis Agassiz on a year-long voyage to Brazil. Perhaps, he thought, this would awaken in him a hidden interest in the natural world. But the excursion only sent the teetering William into a downward spiral of depression and homesickness as he found the collection of samples and specimens to be just as dull as his science studies had been. So he returned to the United States after eight months in South America to resume, and finish, medical school.

All this difficulty with determining his true interests led to a deep depression that William would struggle with throughout his life, most notably after graduating medical school in his late 20s. At age 30 however, now a professor of physiology at Harvard, he suddenly found himself in a job for which he had a natural talent. With a unique mercurial and energetic style of teaching, he soon became popular with the students. After few trips to Europe in the following years to study with a prominent German physician Herman von Helmholtz, he experienced a realization that he was in fact fascinated with psychology. By 1875, as if in tribute to his father's eccentric genes, he'd built the first ever laboratory of *experimental* psychology in the United States and began teaching this subject to Harvard's students, famously remarking at one point that "the first lecture on psychology [he had ever heard was] the first [he] ever gave."

Fifteen years later, William published the work for which he is now most famous, a 1200-page, two-volume tome entitled *The Principles of Psychology*. Written over a 12-year period, *Principles* served as a comprehensive introduction to psychology, incorporating many original views on the subject, including his concept that one's consciousness is a double-sided sense of self, differentiating between objective and subjective personal viewpoints. This kind of extremely open-minded approach to research led him in bizarre directions, such as attending séances to learn more about human psychology in terms of spirituality. William later wrote a more succinct, one-volume version of *Principles* entitled *Psychology: The Briefer Course*. This version was met with only a warm reception, however, some critics commenting that the tone of William's work was far too informal. Renowned psychologist Wilhelm Wundt acerbically remarked, "It is literature – it is beautiful – but it is not psychology."

Later in his life, William branched out from psychology to philosophy as he began lecturing in support of "pragmatism," that is, the belief that ideas are only valid if they are practical and useful in one's life. 1907 saw the publication of his book of the same name *Pragmatism*, an extensive elaboration on this subject.

Now credited as the one who brought both psychology and pragmatism into the public eye, William James's accomplishments in life are awe-inspiring considering he began as an indecisive young man with no idea what he truly wanted, conquering that by allowing his eccentric side to bloom and grow. As he once said, "The best argument I know for an immortal life is the existence of a man who deserves one." Though he may not have acknowledged it himself, William James certainly has come to fit this definition because, true to his words, his ideas and accomplishments immortalized him in the end.

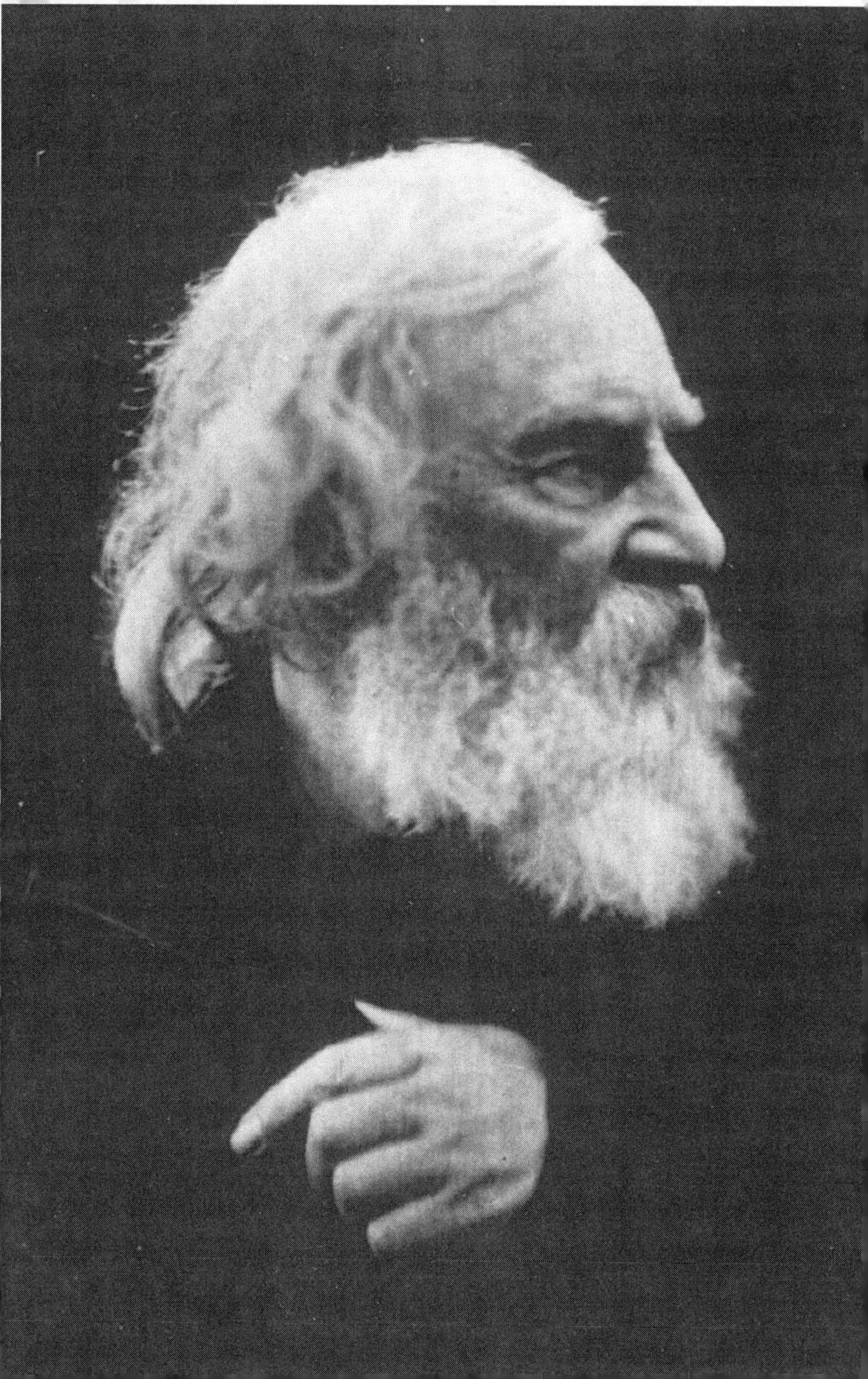

Henry Wadsworth Longfellow: Glass Half-Full

Published in The Concord Journal

We have all heard the name Henry Wadsworth Longfellow, even if many of us have never actually read any of his works. Most would probably nonetheless recognize his most famous works in an instant: *Tales of a Wayside Inn, The Midnight Ride of Paul Revere* and *Song of Hiawatha*. But beyond this high-level recognition, who exactly was Henry?

Born in the wilds of Maine, Henry, whose brother Samuel once described him as both "laid-back" and poetic, graduated from Bowdoin College by age 18, a school that his grandfather helped found and where his father was a trustee. In adult life, Henry would return to Bowdoin to teach, especially after it established a modern languages department and asked him to become its first instructor. This experience coupled with his earlier education contributed to an exposure to a wide variety of literature that ultimately influenced his work. Mythology in particular was a huge influence on Henry, enjoying as a boy books by Washington Irving as well as classics like Don Quixote.

Though a gifted writer early on, Henry's literary prowess was not the main reason he became so successful. His writing style, straightforward and easily understood, made it easier for people to connect with his optimistic, glass half-full perspective. Writing style became a vehicle for a peek into Henry's eccentric, in the sense of supremely positive, frame of mind.

As a result, Henry's work earned him a place alongside the "Fireside Poets" – a group of highly prestigious American poets thought to be on the same level as poets in England. In those days, poetry wasn't considered true art unless it emanated from Europe. Thus Henry, along with William Cullen Bryant, John Greenleaf Whittier, James Russell Lowell, and Oliver Wendell Holmes, Sr., acquired a special status in America on a par with these more respected poets across the pond.

Henry's personal life, however, wasn't quite so successful. He had two wives for starters, both of whom died young. After the death of his first wife Mary Storer Potter (from complications due to a miscarriage), Henry lapsed into a severe depression until he met his second wife, Fanny Appleton. He spent seven years working hard to gain her affection while she resisted his advances every time. But Fanny finally gave in, impressed by his persistence not to mention his early celebrity status. Following their wedding, however, a tragic incident occurred one evening in which sealing wax caught fire and spread to Fanny's clothing. By the next morning Fanny was dead. At this point, Henry couldn't bear to face creating original work any longer, turning instead to a translation of Dante that is still regarded very highly to this day.

Although Henry may have been the most adored poet of his time, not everyone appreciated his work. Transcendentalist writer Margaret Fuller, for one, called Henry's writings "artificial and imitative," adding they possessed "little force." Walt Whitman agreed that Henry tended to imitate other poets though Whitman did admit admiration for Henry's ability to connect so strongly with his audience. Writer Lewis Mumford may have been Henry's toughest critic of all, calling his work "totally devoid" of influence, and claiming that if Longfellow were removed from the course of history… no one would even notice!

Few people today would agree with Mumford's harsh assessment but such indictments do demonstrate how the life of a creative, respected and accomplished writer does not necessarily ensure happiness. The consolation prize may be that Henry's literary achievements continue to be read and enjoyed today, some 150 years later, and continue to generate optimism and reflection.

JAMES GAMBLE ROGERS

James Gamble Rogers: Conventionally Unconventional

Published in The Concord Journal

Reverting to the conventional may not seem to be an unconventional choice, but this was true for architect James Gamble Rogers, born in Kentucky in 1867. Though he designed buildings for many prestigious universities, including Columbia, Northwestern, and the University of Chicago, Rogers is most renowned for his multiple contributions to Yale's campus. A former student of Yale himself, Rogers understood the importance of crafting his architecture to suit the school's image, and he did not need to conform to architectural fads to do so.

Rogers's aesthetic ignored the rising trend of modernism and mainly strove to create a mood. Rather than challenge the public with highly conceptual art, Rogers believed that his architecture should provoke a visceral reaction. Instead of designing buildings marked by the simplicity and functionality of modernism, Rogers opted for the grandeur and distinction of the Gothic and Georgian styles. Yale's Davenport College even features both seemingly incompatible styles – when walking along the sidewalk bordering the college, the exterior is overbearingly Gothic, but once inside the courtyard, the Georgian face of the building reveals itself.

When designing for various universities, Rogers kept in mind that these institutions needed to project an air of stateliness, and so he used these recognizable architectural benchmarks to achieve this effect. However, Rogers did not overlook advances in architectural technology either, commonly using (for example) hidden steel bars to strengthen his buildings' infrastructures.

A set of strong beliefs drove Rogers forward as an architect. For one thing, he felt that all buildings should look older than they actually were in an effort to immortalize them. Rogers thus frequently poured acid on his buildings' façades in order to achieve this "aged" effect. When working at Yale, Rogers also held the conviction that a religious building, say a chapel or a cathedral, should mark the center of the campus. However, Yale ultimately rejected Rogers' plans to build either a chapel or Yale's divinity school on the central green, instructing him instead to build a library there. While other architects might have admitted defeat at this point, Rogers did not passively concede to their demands. Instead, he forged ahead to design and construct the picturesque Sterling Memorial Library in the style of a Gothic cathedral, with card catalogues in place of pews and an oak librarian's desk in place of an altar. The "religious" center of the university, fittingly enough, would forever be its intellectual center.

In 1947, James Gamble Rogers died in New York, leaving behind an impressive volume of work to immortalize not merely his buildings but his name as well. In his 80 years of life, Rogers created his own brand of conventionally unconventional architecture, his legacy speaking for itself through his work.

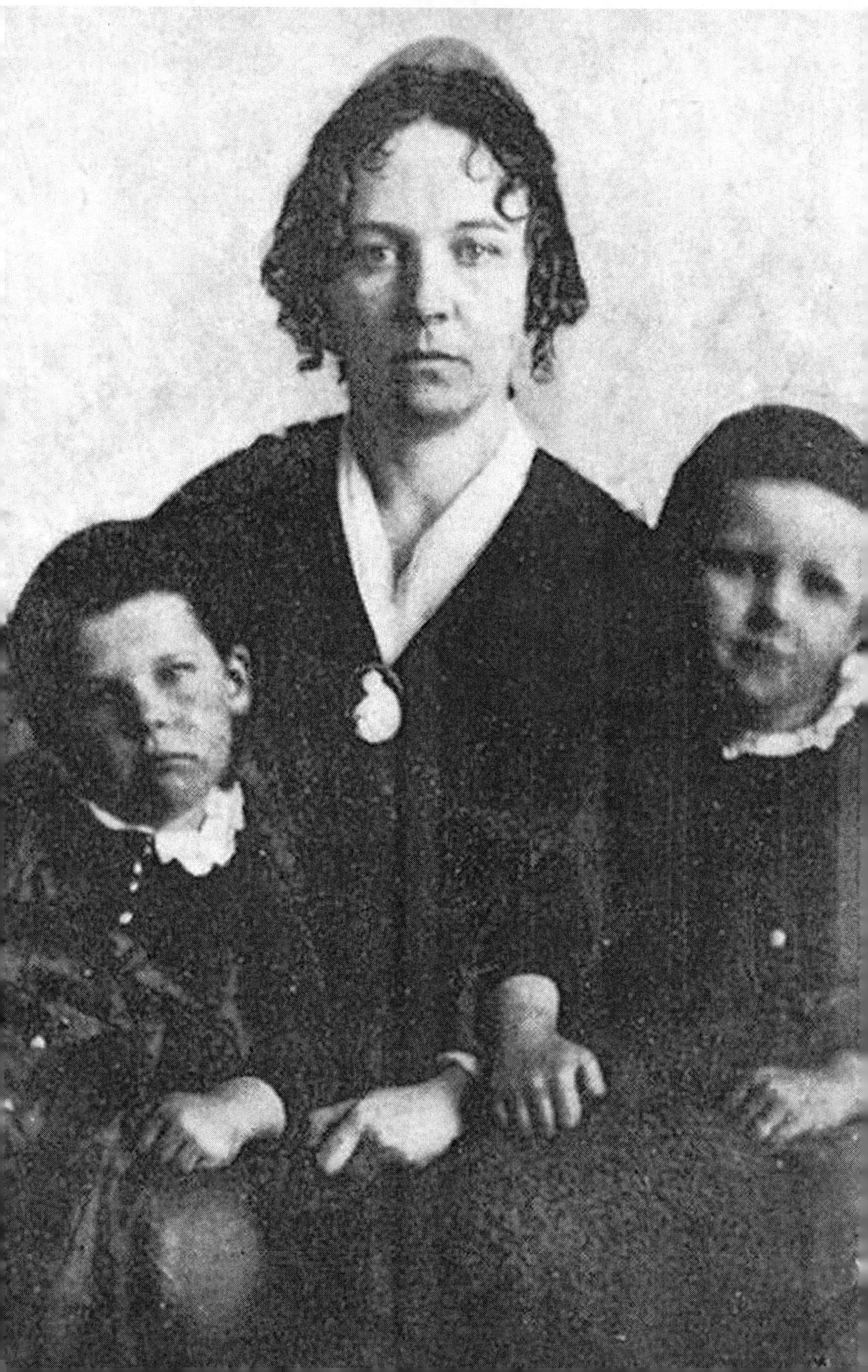

Elizabeth Cady Stanton: Her Iron Will Opened Doors

Published in The The Concord Journal

Elizabeth Cady Stanton, a talented writer unafraid to speak her mind, was a vital member of the women's rights movement and contributed to the intellectual growth of our new nation. Born on November 12, 1815 in Johnstown, New York, a community that Elizabeth soon found out favored men over women, she excelled in school despite this handicap, even winning a prize in her Greek class. Upon showing her father her award, he remarked, "Oh, I wish you were a boy!" But rather than dispiriting her, comments such as this fueled the fire that drove Elizabeth later in life to demand rights and recognition for all women.

Elizabeth and others chose to hold a women's rights convention in Seneca Falls in July of 1848. For the convention, she wrote a piece called the "Declaration of Sentiments" with twelve accompanying resolutions. Her document was closely modeled after the Declaration of Independence, beginning "We hold these truths to be self evident, that all men *and women* are created equal." Elizabeth delivered this speech at the convention, shocking the crowd with the idea that women should have the right to vote as this type of societal modification was unheard of up to that time. However, the crowd came to accept such radical ideas after hearing more heartfelt speeches. With the influence of Elizabeth and others present at Seneca Falls, the women's rights movement had officially begun.

Elizabeth wrote many speeches about feminism, including "The Degradation of Self" and "The Solitude of Self," both written in 1892. Often, these speeches were delivered by Susan B. Anthony rather than Elizabeth herself. While both women were focused on suffrage, Elizabeth also strongly fought for divorce reform, religious reform, and equal educational and job opportunities for both sexes. Meanwhile, Susan was primarily focused on suffrage. While women's rights were Elizabeth's first priority, she also believed that African Americans deserved equality and, as a result, during the Civil War, she worked tirelessly with abolitionists to abolish slavery. However, she decided to part ways with abolitionist groups after the war when they began favoring voting rights for blacks over women.

In 1878, Elizabeth took direct aim at this by persuading Aaron A. Sargent, a senator from California, to sponsor an amendment on women's suffrage to the Constitution. Though it initially failed, this amendment was re-introduced every year thereafter until Congress finally approved it in 1919, making it the 19th amendment to the Constitution in 1920. Sadly, Elizabeth herself never lived to see the day when she would be able to vote, her life ending 18 years before in 1902. From 1881 to 1886 however, she spent much time writing the first three volumes of *A History of Woman Suffrage* with Susan B. Anthony, then in the 1890s, her autobiography, *80 Years and More*, as well as *The Degradation of Self* and *The Solitude of Self*. Although Elizabeth's body was aging in those years, her mind and soul never once stopped working toward her goal of equal rights for women.

If eccentricity means "separated from the normal," Elizabeth Cady Stanton might fit such a definition as she never once reconsidered her opposition to "normal society's" categorization of women as second-class citizens. Throughout her life she always remained steadfastly optimistic and hopeful that women would one day gain the rights they deserved. Though she passed away before she could see any governmental recognition of her ideas, she will always be honored as a key figure who set new precedents for activists and laid the groundwork for modern feminism.

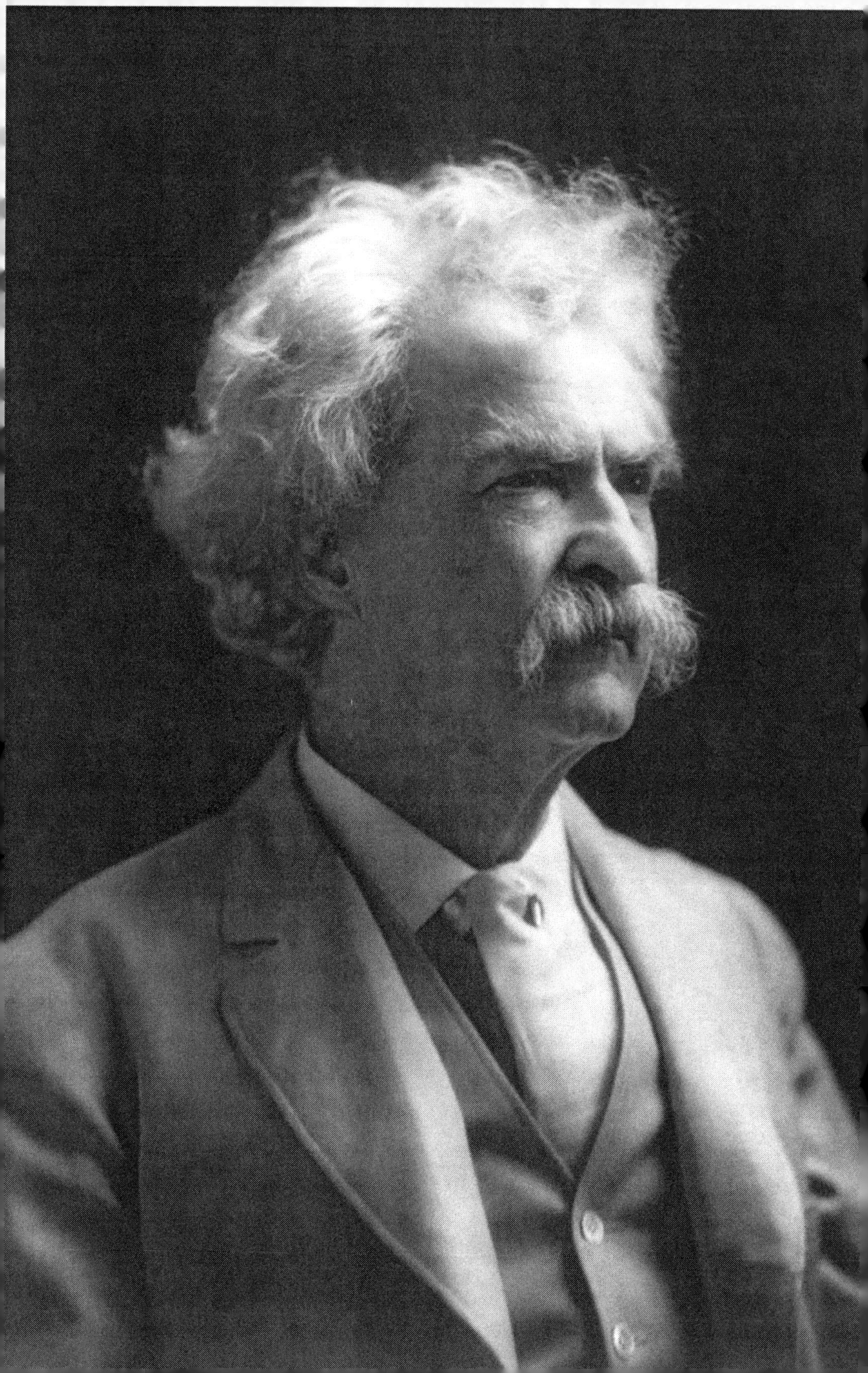

Mark Twain: Not Necessarily Safe to Travel

Published in The Concord Journal

The name "Samuel Langhorn Clemens" is a mouthful of syllables nowhere near as easy to remember as short punchy pen names like Thoreau, Alcott, Emerson or Hawthorne. Perhaps this helps understand why Sam Clemens elected to adopt the more notable nom de plume of Mark Twain, taken from his earlier career, when the time came for him to begin writing stories and books. Born in 1835 in Missouri, Twain/Clemens had been greatly affected by the culture of the Mississippi River, dreaming as a boy of one day becoming a steamboat river pilot. At 22, while working as a steamboat apprentice in St. Louis, he learned that an essential part of driving a boat is awareness of the river's depths at all times. To determine that the water is at least 12 feet deep and therefore safe for your boat to travel is to "mark twain."

Later, in 1861, Twain relocated to Virginia City, Nevada where he began to work as a journalist. Initially as a correspondent for a San Francisco newspaper *The Call,* he eventually decided to leave Virginia City for fear of legal repercussions after he challenged the editor of a rival publication to a duel! Escaping to San Francisco, he soon grew bored of his work as a full time reporter for *The Call* and quit to contribute to a variety of newspapers and literary magazines. However, that too needed to end after about a year as many of his articles aimed his flaring temper at San Francisco's police department, thus catching too much of the wrong kind of attention from local authorities. In the safety of Tuolumne Foothills in California, where he attempted to do some mining, Twain retold on paper a story he heard from the locals, titling his retelling "The Celebrated Jumping Frog of Calaveras County." This was his first taste of success in literature, finally bringing the name Mark Twain into the public eye.

Although he went on to write hugely popular books such as *The Adventures of Tom Sawyer* in 1876 and *Huckleberry Finn* in 1885, Twain nonetheless found himself deeply in debt. A big reason for this was that he had invested large amounts of money in a new version of the typesetting machine. Convinced that this invention was a stroke of genius, he expected that he would not need to write another word to sustain himself once this remarkable new typesetter hit the market. Income from the profits of such a can't-miss new product would be more than enough to keep him afloat financially and settle all his debts.

Unfortunately, Twain's master plan went horribly wrong. He had also founded a publishing company that was losing money, which forced him to stop contributing money on the typesetter project so that he could shift attention to saving his company. But by this time he had spent more than $200,000 on the typesetter, leaving him with not nearly enough money to also save the publishing company. The majority of Twain's income had thus disappeared, plummeting him into a debt from he could never recover.

Ever true to his sense of humor and irony, Twain, born in the same year that Halley's Comet had appeared in the night skies, famously remarked in 1909: "I came in with Halley's Comet in 1835. It is coming again next year, and I expect to go out with it…The Almighty has said, no doubt: 'Now here are these two unaccountable freaks; they came in together, they must go out together.'" Eerily enough, his prediction came true. Mark Twain died in 1910, exactly one day after Halley's Comet returned. Luckily for us on the planet Earth, Twain's literature and legacy did not disappear with him, staying around much longer than the famous comet.

F. Wayland

Francis Wayland: Wise, Unconventional and Majestic

Published in The Concord Journal

Brown University's image as one of the most forward-thinking schools in the country was perpetuated by its notable president Francis Wayland, born in New York City in 1796, a man who cycled through a variety of professions before arriving in the field of education. At university, he studied medicine, but he left this career path behind and decided he would become a minister. Although he could not financially afford to fully complete his studies of theology, Wayland nonetheless went on to serve as the pastor of Boston's First Baptist Church for five years. This position brought Wayland's name to the attention of the staff at Brown University, who had also been aware of Wayland's work as a professor at Union College. Because of his growing reputation as an innovative thinker, they promptly selected Wayland to become the next president of their institution. Wayland went on to serve as Brown's president from 1827 to 1855.

Wayland's background in philosophy informed the way he looked at the American collegiate system. He was known to be unconventional in his teaching methods, insisting for instance that textbooks should not be brought into classrooms, in an effort to shift learning away from recitation and towards student-driven discussion. Additionally, Wayland was skilled at keeping his students in line by maintaining stern discipline while also acting wise and majestic at the same time. He would for example often make memorable philosophical declarations when students visited him in his office, for which students greatly respected his wisdom.

Wayland was also memorable for a slightly more unusual mannerism: spitting tobacco! He would habitually spit on a designated mat next to his desk before delivering the daily prayers to the student body. At one of Brown's "semi-annual exhibitions," a student even added to the program that "Dr. Wayland, with his accustomed accuracy, will now snuff a candle with tobacco juice at a distance of five paces."

Having traveled to the United Kingdom and France to study educational systems outside of the United States, Wayland ultimately gathered sufficient research to write *Thoughts on the Present Collegiate System* in the United States in which he asserted that most American universities did not provide enough depth of learning for their students, most classes barely scratching the surface of what students could potentially learn about a subject. As a result, Wayland called for major overhauls at Brown in particular.

Almost inevitably, his plans were met with opposition, seeming impractical to more conventional minds of the time. To shift the climate, Wayland threatened to resign as president if his curriculum reforms were not attempted. This ultimatum made the task appear slightly more manageable for those Brown Corporation directors who, in the end, did not want to see him go. To prevent his leaving, many reluctantly agreed to give the proposed changes a chance.

Wayland next presented the Corporation with a comprehensive report, fittingly titled *Report to the Corporation of Brown University on changes in the system of collegiate education*, and by doing so firmly ushered in a more progressive outlook on education.

His "New Curriculum" was created based on many of the same beliefs that pervade Brown's present day open curriculum. He famously remarked that Brown's "various courses should be so arranged, that in so far as it is practical, every student might study what he chose, all that he chose, and nothing but what he chose." Wayland also hoped to provide education to lower social classes interested in various trades who may not have been able to afford education elsewhere. He believed it "eminently unjust practically to exclude the largest classes of the community from an opportunity of acquiring that knowledge."

Though he died way back in 1865, Wayland's name today is still widely revered by the Brown community as the one brave individual most responsible for moving the school forward in its educational process and academic ideology.

ARTS/ENTERTAINMENT

ACADEMY AWARD® NOMINEE
NATALIE PORTMAN
VINCENT CASSEL   MILA KUNIS

BLACK SWAN

A FILM BY DARREN ARONOFSKY
THE DIRECTOR OF THE WRESTLER AND REQUIEM FOR A DREAM

FOX SEARCHLIGHT PICTURES PRESENTS IN ASSOCIATION WITH CROSS CREEK PICTURES
NATALIE PORTMAN VINCENT CASSEL MILA KUNIS "BLACK SWAN" BARBARA HERSHEY AND WINONA RYDER
JIM BLACK AND GABE HILFER CLINT MANSELL ANDREW WEISBLUM, A.C.E. THÉRÈSE DePREZ
MATTHEW LIBATIQUE, ASC MIKE MEDAVOY ARNOLD W. MESSER BRIAN OLIVER SCOTT FRANKLIN
ANDRÉS HEINZ MARK HEYMAN AND ANDRÉS HEINZ AND JOHN McLAUGHLIN DARREN ARONOFSKY

THIS FALL
www.blackswan2010.com

Black Swan: Film Review

Published by CCHS student newspaper The Voice

Striving for perfection is a common struggle among artists, but sometimes it becomes difficult to recognize when one has crossed the line into an unhealthy obsession. Audiences who attend a showing of *Black Swan* will have absolutely no trouble realizing that protagonist Nina Sayers (Natalie Portman) has haphazardly pole-vaulted over this line to the point of no return as she prepares herself to play the lead role in the famous ballet, *Swan Lake*. Straight away, it is clear that her technical skills are unparalleled – the role of the delicate, innocent white swan would suit her remarkably well. However, French choreographer Thomas (Vincent Cassel) believes that Nina is far too innocent to convincingly portray the seductive black swan. Her dreams of achieving perfection have prevented her from dancing with fluid, free emotion. Since the roles of the white swan and the black swan are traditionally played by the same ballerina, Thomas encourages Nina to embrace recklessness and wild darkness in order to improve her performance as the black swan. The film tracks Nina's resulting descent into madness as she takes his advice slightly too much to heart.

Viewers should know this is not a fluffy movie about ballet, and, quite honestly, I cannot remember a single scene where I felt at ease. Director Darren Aronofsky creates the perfect atmosphere for the film; it is shot very claustrophobically, which makes it clear that this is a story told only from Nina's perspective. Abrupt cuts to bizarre, disturbing images add to the tension, making this a very successful psychological thriller. The ambiguous nature of events is also fascinating – the film arrives at a certain point where one can't be sure if certain scenes are actually happening in reality or only in Nina's head – making the movie perfect for multiple viewings. The artistic value of the film is outstanding, and it is no surprise that it is nominated for four Golden Globes.

That said, the film's tension builds to incalculable heights, so much that occasionally it can border on comedy. Certain scenes seemed so insane to the point where the entire cinema actually burst out laughing. However, this does not affect the overall artistic value of the movie. In fact, comic relief was welcome every so often to distract from the intensity.

Not for the faint-hearted or those who want to spend an idle Saturday afternoon with a light drama, *Black Swan* is a lesson in taking perfection too far. Being a bit of a perfectionist myself, I am thankful to remind myself on a daily basis: *At least I'm not Nina Sayers.*

Final Grade: A-

F. SCOTT FITZGERALD

THE GREAT GATSBY

Boats Against the Current: The Role of the Green Light in *The Great Gatsby*

Published by Booklore

The concept of a flawless future is one that most people aspire to but can never fully obtain. This idea of completely achieving one's dreams, a facet of the classic "American Dream," is central to the plot of F. Scott Fitzgerald's novel *The Great Gatsby*. The book follows Jay Gatsby as he struggles to pursue his ambitions in life, which lead him to Daisy Buchanan. Despite the fact that Gatsby's relationship with Daisy ended five years earlier, he is determined that he can revive the past and, in so doing, live the life he always dreamed of. From his house, Gatsby often sees a green light at the end of Daisy's dock, which is a crucial motif in the book. The green light symbolizes Gatsby's hopes and dreams of an ideal life, yet even though he ceaselessly reaches out in the direction of this guiding light, he is oblivious to the unattainable nature of his wishes.

While Gatsby is pursuing Daisy, the green light calls out to him as a representation of the future he longs for. The introduction of Gatsby's character in the novel serves as an indication of his major conflict. Nick catches sight of Gatsby standing alone in his yard one summer night, "stretch[ing] his arms toward the dark water in a curious way" while "trembling" (20-21). Nick's eyes drift across the water in the direction of Gatsby's arms and he is able to discern "nothing except a single green light, minute and far way" (21). Later, Nick discovers that the green light shines from the end of Daisy's dock. However, Gatsby reaches not only for Daisy herself but for his idea of Daisy and the utopian future he associates with her. Looking across the water to the light, Gatsby's dreams appear so attainable, yet just beyond his grasp. After Jordan informs Nick that Gatsby bought his house specifically so that Daisy would be across the water, he muses that "it had not merely been the stars to which [Gatsby] had aspired on that June night" (78). In a sense, Gatsby is reaching for the stars as well. He heavily idealizes all of his dreams and builds them up to a stellar level. If he reunites with Daisy, Gatsby has no doubt that his life will simply fall into place, his visions of an immaculate, flawless future finally coming alive. Even though it becomes clear that Gatsby's dreams are more corrupt than they seem, he endlessly thirsts for the impeccable future embodied by the green light.

In addition, it is worth noting that the green color of the light itself manifests Gatsby's envy of what lies across the water. Gatsby's jealousy of Tom, Daisy's husband, is palpable throughout the novel, as Gatsby strongly desires everything about the life Tom lives. His marriage to Daisy only fuels Gatsby's state of mental hysteria. Nick quickly realizes that Gatsby "wanted nothing less of Daisy than that she should go to Tom and say: 'I never loved you'" (109). In the ideal future Gatsby envisions, Tom never existed. Everything is exactly the way it was five years earlier, before Gatsby left Daisy to go off to war. Blinded by his complete attachment to the idea of Daisy, Gatsby convinces himself that Daisy never fell out of love with him, believing Tom to be a mere aberration from Daisy's true feelings.

The green color of the light also connects to the green color of the money and wealth Gatsby has longed for his entire life. Even at a young age, Gatsby *incessantly* dreams of "a universe of ineffable gaudiness" (99) and excess that he wishes he could indulge in, a consequence of being raised in a poor household. Near the end of the novel, it is revealed that money, class, and social status are the true reasons why Gatsby pursues Daisy in the first place. Because of his modest upbringing, Gatsby feels that he has "no real right" (149) to Daisy and perceives her in terms of her "value" (149). The sumptuousness of Daisy's life lures Gatsby in, drawing him to associate a life with Daisy with a life of luxury and money. Gatsby's financially-oriented goals lead him to pursue Daisy so persistently, the idea of Daisy and the wealth she represents epitomizing his visions of perfection.

Though Gatsby concentrates all of his energy on attaining this ideal future, it escapes him that his dreams are actually unattainable. Nick comments that Gatsby "talked a lot about the past, and [he] gathered that he wanted to recover something, some idea of himself perhaps, that had gone into loving Daisy" (110). Gatsby spends his time focusing on a phase of his life that has already passed – he recalls the glorified flawlessness of that time and wants nothing more than to re-create it. His perceptions of reality are skewed towards his obsession with reviving this memory, and then fails to pick up on the fact that his dreams only exist as a memory. In the beginning of the book, the waves of the Sound are the only barrier between Gatsby and that elusive green light, much like time separates him from his ambitions. At the end of the book, Nick looks out at the Sound reflecting upon Gatsby's ubiquitous hope in his dreams. He notes that though Gatsby's "dream must have seemed so close that he could hardly fail to grasp it" (180), he did not understand that it had already drifted away five years earlier. Similar to the waves of the Sound, these moments in time drift past before one can realize it. The cornerstone of life is its transitory nature. Gatsby loses himself to visions of his glorified past, separated from the object of his obsession by subtly elapsed time.

As the book draws to a close, Nick elaborates on the significance of the green light. The last line of the book summarizes Gatsby's struggle over the course of the book: "So we beat on, boats against the current, borne back ceaselessly into the past" (180). Not only is this a stunning final sentence, it also ties the book together very effectively. Gatsby's dreams send him delving into his past and attempting to transfer these dreams to his future. Though the green light represents everything that was pure about the future for him, it directs him backwards in life instead of forwards. Gatsby's boat has already passed by Daisy, and he never comes to understand that it is time to move on. Though everyone continues to drift in their respective boats towards that ever-unreachable future, fighting the current brings one a step backward. Allowing the current to take control may lead the boat into uncharted waters, but letting life plot its own course also may make that elusive green light more clearly defined than ever.

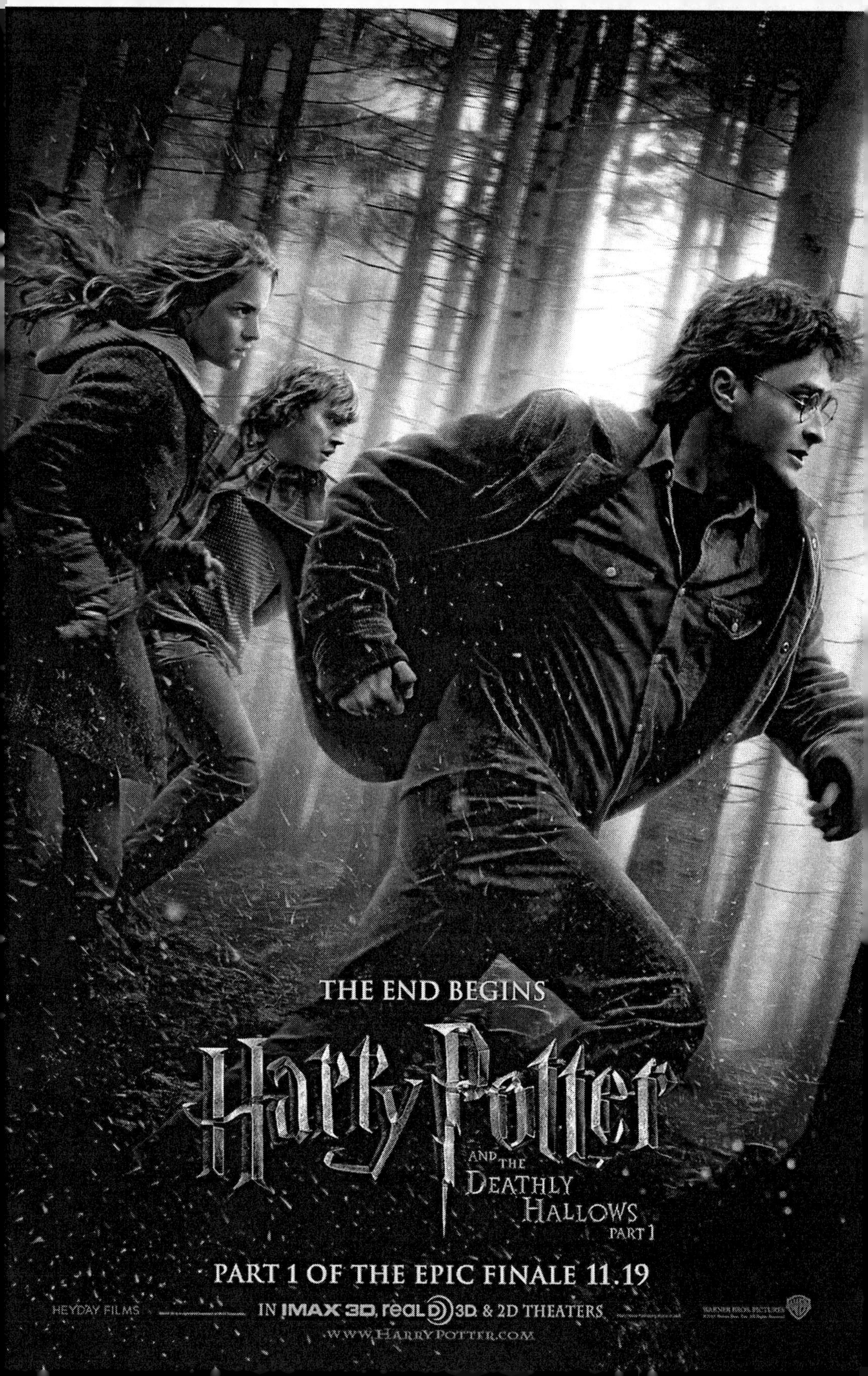

THE END BEGINS
Harry Potter
AND THE
DEATHLY
HALLOWS
PART 1
PART 1 OF THE EPIC FINALE 11.19
HEYDAY FILMS
IN IMAX 3D, realD 3D & 2D THEATERS
WARNER BROS. PICTURES
WWW.HARRYPOTTER.COM

Harry Potter and the Deathly Hallows – Part I: Film Review

Published by CCHS student newspaper The Voice

"These are dark times; there is no denying," booms the Minister of Magic Rufus Scrimgeour in the tone-setting opening scene of *Harry Potter and the Deathly Hallows: Part I.* True to the book, the first part of the film adaptation is the darkest film installment yet. It wastes no time summarizing previous events (and rightly so – if you haven't read the books, shame on you) and jumps right back into the chaotic world of Harry Potter in the aftermath of Dumbledore's death. As usual, the film has generated much hype from die-hard fans, and it fails to disappoint those who have re-read the entire series more times than they can count.

Despite the fact that certain details have been overlooked or altered, it is apparent that director David Yates and co. have attempted to make an adaptation that stays true to the J.K. Rowling novels. It was a wise decision to split the book into two movies – the final book is packed from start to finish with important events that serve as a fitting final send-off to Harry. The acting is top-notch as usual – particularly poignant is a movie-specific scene where Harry and Hermione are dancing to a Nick Cave song in their tent. It brings to the foreground one of the most moving aspects of the series, the friendship among the trio of Harry, Ron, and Hermione amidst a world of chaos and darkness. Another surprising highlight was the re-telling of the Story of the Three Brothers, which conjures up a Tim Burton-esque visual interlude to the action. Brief breaks such as these pace the plot of the movie and are unexpected surprises for Potter obsessives.

Since most know the plot of the series like the back of their hand, the real mystery about the film is its ending point. At what point would screenwriter Steve Kloves decide to split the book into two parts? Without giving too much away, the ending will not disappoint – it is a satisfying enough cliffhanger without leaving too many ends untied. I was surprised that about two thirds of the book was covered in this movie, but it makes sense that more time should ultimately be spent on the final encounter between Harry and Voldemort. All fans can do now is wait impatiently until July, when *Deathly Hallows: Part II* is released, providing a bittersweet finale to the beloved series. But these fans likely will not wait idly – this movie warrants at least three more return trips to the local IMAX theater.

Final Grade: A+

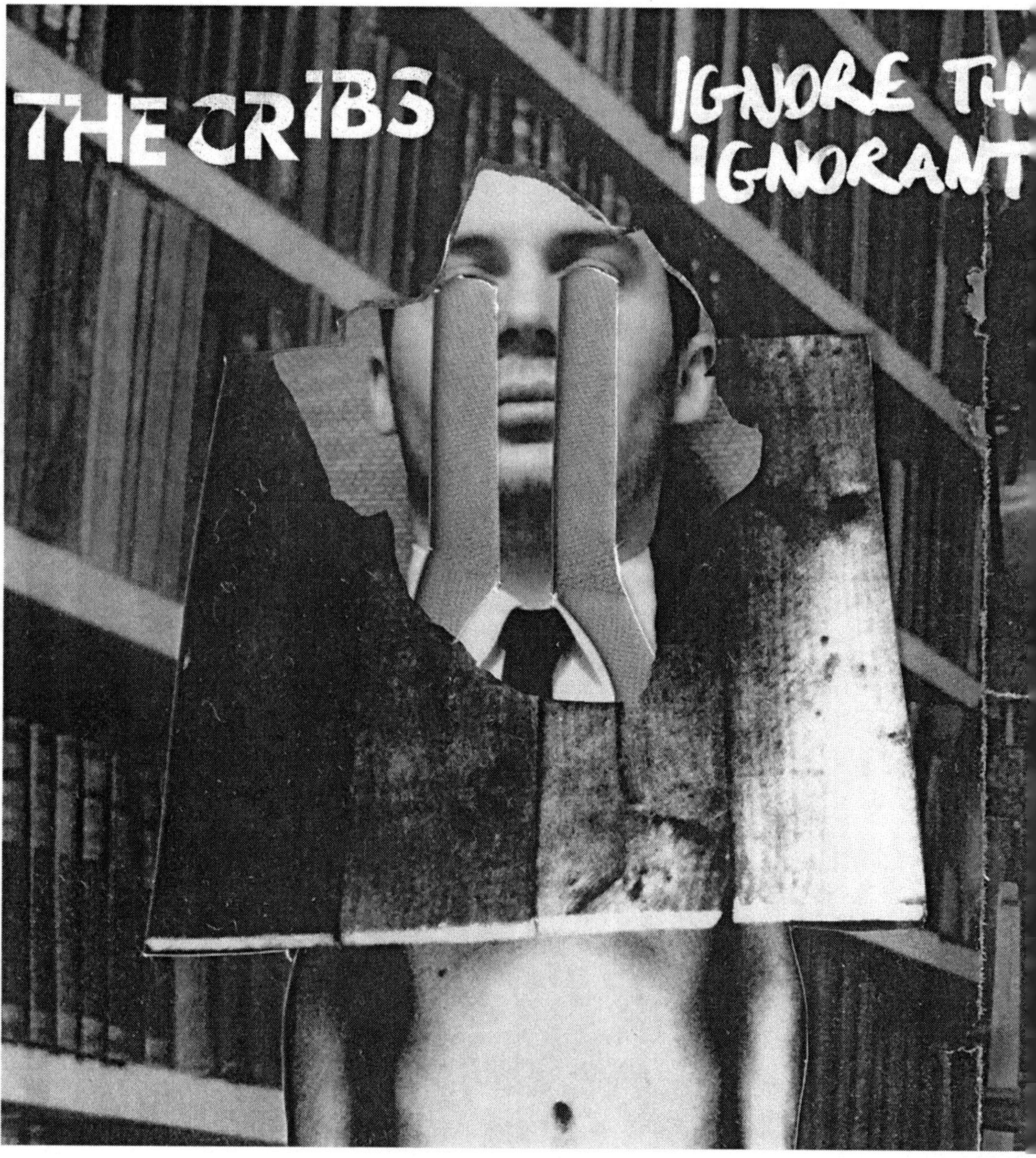
THE CRIBS
IGNORE TH
IGNORANT

Ignore the Ignorant by The Cribs: CD Review

Published by The Real Musician

For a band like The Cribs that was self-proclaimed to be "a band of brothers" for ages, it was strange news to hear that they had recruited an additional full-time member. Even more surprisingly, Ryan, Gary and Ross Jarman, the three original Cribs, were not only adding a new guitar player but they were adding *Johnny Marr*. Yes, *that* Johnny Marr, guitarist for indie legends The Smiths and, more recently, Modest Mouse. This definitely raised the stakes for the fourth Cribs album, *Ignore the Ignorant* – not only did it need to push the band to the next level, it still needed to sound like The Cribs so that the addition of someone with such a well-established style did not alienate the core fan base. As a huge fan of both The Cribs and all of Johnny Marr's work, I knew the album would be good, but I had no idea just where it would go.

The album opens with the guitar attack of "We Were Aborted," taking the blend of guitar hooks and soaring, anthemic choruses that is The Cribs' trademark to that aforementioned next level. Ryan's raw, emotional vocal delivery seems more on point than ever before. Fast-paced and aggressive, the energy of the song is sure to translate amazingly well in the live environment, especially at the riot-like shows The Cribs are notorious for instigating. "Cheat on Me," the lead single, slows the album's heart rate ever so slightly with lighter, intertwining guitars, yet still sends chills down the spine. Atop the soundscape, Gary takes vocals on this one, his lyrics still clever without being overly poetic. The first few songs come across as distinctly Cribs, with some added sophistication – a natural progression for the band, even if somewhat expected.

Track four is the point where the album begins to separate itself as a true masterpiece. "City of Bugs" begins innocuously enough with feedback-y guitar but when the rhythm locks into place, it is clear that this is no Cribs-by-numbers album. The lighter verses give way with massive pickslides to a wall of guitars, the musical equivalent of that first drop on a roller coaster. Everything lines up perfectly—drum, bass, guitar, vocals, and lyrics—all with a newfound style and depth. Unlike anything The Cribs have ever touched on before, the six-minute epic takes the band in a fresher direction while nonetheless fitting in effortlessly with the rest of their canon.

The songs flow into one another especially well, fitting together as an album rather than as just a collection of songs. The title track stands out among the fray, seeming to sum up what the band tries to convey in their 47-minute musical statement of a record. This serves as an excellent representation of their new sound, entangled riffs forming a background for "throwing England to the dogs." The CD finishes with "Stick to Yr Guns," a mellower end for this adrenaline rush in audio but still a fitting bit of closure. Its momentum gradually builds to become much more than a final ballad and one of the best songs on the record.

The Cribs have written some of their career's best. The doors that the new material has opened overshadow the album's, in essence, supreme excellence. Johnny Marr's guitar, while distinguishable, serves the purpose of the songs without eclipsing the original Cribs. *Ignore the Ignorant* is an unexpected triumph. With this record as its starting point, the possibilities for album number five are enough to make all Cribs fans everywhere tap their Converses impatiently on the floor before remembering they can just tap along to this fourth album in the meantime and make the wait for #5 tolerable.

the office

Life Without Michael: Reflections on "The Office" in Transition

Published by CEO Refresher

"This is going to feel so good, getting this thing off my chest." He hands his microphone pack over to the film crew, cutting off all audio. He spreads his arms and delivers a soundless final remark: *That's what she said.*

Along with 8.4 million other viewers[1], I couldn't help but crack a smile at Steve Carell's fitting final line as Michael Scott on "The Office." Despite the season-long buildup to Carell's departure, it was still incredibly difficult to accept that Michael Scott would never again return to the offices of Dunder Mifflin's Scranton branch. Even as I type this, I still feel an overwhelming sense of denial that Carell has actually left. I still cling to a completely irrational shred of hope that I will turn on NBC next Thursday at 9 PM and see Michael Scott up to his usual hijinks. That completely oblivious and proud smirk of Michael's was the perfect capper to my Thursday night.

Throughout my formative years, "The Office" has been one of the main constants in my life. I still fondly look back on that fateful summer night when, aged 11, I was first introduced to the show. As I watched Michael Scott and his co-workers play a cringe-worthy game of basketball against the Dunder Mifflin warehouse staff, I could not contain myself, choking on gasps of laughter. Every half-second sequence was just as insane as the last, from Michael's sidekick Dwight Schrute dribbling water into a protective face

---

[1] Guthrie, Marisa. "Steve Carell's 'Office' farewell boosts ratings." April 29, 2011. May 1, 2011. http://www.reuters.com/article/2011/04/29/us-office-idUSTRE73S0KP20110429

mask to out-of-shape Kevin sinking every shot he took from halfway down the court. What was this madness? At the center of the chaos was the one and only Michael Scott, humming Harlem Globetrotters-esque jazz music and spinning around on one knee while dribbling the basketball. He clearly existed in his own selective version of reality. As an impressionable preteen, I was excited by the off-color nature of Carell's comedy. I was just old enough to appreciate the uncomfortable, politically incorrect asides that were intrinsic to Michael Scott. "The Office" felt fresh, unique, and certainly more mature than any of the other shows I watched. It aired at *9:30 PM* – that's practically *midnight* when you're in grade school.

Although only six years have passed, it feels like an entire lifetime since I first met the crew at Dunder Mifflin. I have actually evolved into a somewhat mature human being since then – I am gearing up to apply to colleges, I know that I prefer MSNBC to Fox News, and I can operate a motor vehicle. If I were to take a trip back in time to see my 11-year-old self, we would have little in common – I didn't even have an *iPod* yet – but if we were to sit down and watch an episode of "The Office," we would understand how we could possibly share the same genetic coding.

Sure, I've changed my hairstyle and explored new interests, but I have never lost interest in "The Office." A new episode was something to look forward to, something dependable. "The Office" was the unofficial beginning of the weekend, consistent hilarity guaranteed. While the show did develop over the years, it never lost its heart: a dysfunctional group of office workers that functioned as one large family. And the boss of the unit, Michael Scott, was always the leader of this mad troupe. Despite his immaturity and ignorant remarks, it seemed impossible not to sympathize with Michael. At the root of his over-the-top improv stunts, Michael was a character desperate to be appreciated by others, buying himself a Spencer Gifts mug sporting the phrase "World's Best Boss" and attempting to embody it through his bizarre yet sincere behavior. Ensemble piece or not, Michael has been the most important cog in the Dunder Mifflin machine, leading the weekly action and representing the Scranton branch.

Now, though, Michael has moved on. He has left Dunder Mifflin to start a new life with fiancée Holly Flax. Although this is a fitting send-off to Michael's character – he finally got his happy ending – I, along with several million other viewers, realized the bittersweet importance of this episode.

Suddenly, "The Office" is changing. Completely. Though it is true that "The Office" has found its strength as an ensemble piece, Michael Scott's character is irreplaceable. Who else could accidentally burn their foot on a George Foreman grill? Who else would create an Oscar-like awards ceremony to celebrate his co-workers, handing out awards such as "Whitest Sneakers" and "Bushiest Beaver"? Who else would arrange for the entire staff to drive up to Niagara Falls to attend token "Office" couple Jim and Pam's wedding ceremony? A "changing of the guard," in this case, cannot capture the true essence of Michael's character. Unlike the paper he sells, Michael's character cannot be Xeroxed.

At the same time, it's essential that the loyal fanbase keep in mind that "forever changed" does not necessarily mean "forever unwatchable." Other TV shows have found success in replacing cast members without a decline in quality. "Saturday Night Live," for example, has survived for more than thirty years on the basis of a rotating cast. English national treasure "Doctor Who" has cycled through eleven different actors in the all-important lead role over its 48 year run. The show still boasts a rabid fanbase and critical adoration, with 2011 BAFTA nominations for lead actor Matt Smith and writer Steven Moffat.[2] Carell's departure marks not only the end of an "Office" era but also an unopened ream of Dunder Mifflin paper. A carbon copy replacement of Michael Scott would be impossible, but the addition of a new regional manager could add new blood to the cast and reinvigorate plot lines. Ricky Gervais, the creator of the original "Office" series on BBC and producer of the American reboot, even sent Carell an email to tell him that he was "doing the right thing. As a producer, I was expected to try and stop him because he's a big part of it, [but] you know, it can survive. Whether it should or not, I don't know."[3]

This gray area is what tortures "Office" fans the most. While the show could continue to thrive on unique story lines and off-color humor, it is equally possible that Michael's absence could be so noticeable as to distract from the positive. Even if a worthy "replacement" does join the ranks of

---

[2] Plunkett, John. "BAFTAs battle between Doctor Who and Sherlock." April 26, 2011. May 4, 2011.
http://www.guardian.co.uk/tv-and-radio/2011/apr/26/baftas-battle-doctor-who-sherlock

[3] Gervais, Ricky. Interview with Piers Morgan. Piers Morgan Tonight. CNN, New York, 21 January 2011.

Dunder Mifflin Scranton, something may still be lacking. It's difficult to imagine this new chapter of "The Office" living up to Michael's legacy. However, the producers and cast will certainly attempt to do so, and I owe them my dedication as a loyal viewer. Despite my pessimism, I'm interested to see the new direction of the show.

As Michael himself once said, "Sometimes I start a sentence and I don't even know where it's going. I just hope that I find it along the way." I'm hoping for the same.

the CATCHER in the RYE

a novel by **J. D. SALINGER**

Life in Transition: Holden Caulfield's Journey into Adulthood

Published by Booklore

While growing up is inevitable, coming to terms with the process remains elusive at best. Such is the struggle of Holden Caulfield, the protagonist and walking personification of teenage angst in J.D. Salinger's *The Catcher in the Rye*. Holden Caulfield is not a typical 16-year-old, but his feelings of alienation in a world of "phonies" as well as his fear of the passage from childhood to adulthood echo through the halls of most modern high schools. Holden faces an acute identity crisis—he does not understand the world around him, yet, more importantly, he does not really want to. After an emotional nosedive highlighted by an expulsion from Pencey Prep, Holden checks into The Edmont Hotel and wanders the environs of Manhattan for three days. However, as Holden's adventure progresses, he slowly begins to bridge the gap between the innocence of childhood and the onset of adulthood. The second-to-last chapter of *The Catcher in the Rye* follows Holden as a few significant events contribute to his gain of personal closure regarding the loss of innocence between childhood and adulthood, one of the book's universal themes.

Holden's walk on Fifth Avenue at the start of the chapter symbolizes his many struggles throughout the book related to his journey into adulthood. As his feet carry him down the endless blocks, he becomes increasingly panicked with each step, remarking to himself, "I had this feeling that I'd never get to the other side of the street. I thought I'd just go down, down,

down, and nobody'd ever see me again" (256). This fear of "falling" as related to the title *The Catcher in the Rye* is a play on a Robert Burns poem and sheds light on Holden's ideal purpose in a world full of "phonies." Holden literally wants to "catch" the children as they plummet into adulthood. Holden, like any other teenager, is frightened of growing up. He knows that no one is at the bottom of the metaphorical cliff with open arms to catch him as he falls, and that terrifies him more than anything. This fear of the edge of the cliff pushes Holden to walk on the line between childhood and adulthood without committing to either side, paralleling his sprints from block to block. Additionally, Holden clings to one of the only thoughts that he could ever find comforting for strength – the memory of his brother, Allie. As he runs, he "make[s] believe he [is] talking to [his] brother Allie" (257) and thanks him when he crosses the street safely. In a sense, Holden regards Allie as his catcher at the bottom of the cliff. He keeps Allie's catcher's mitt with him at all times, and it is clear Allie's death affected him in an irreversible manner that made it extremely difficult for him to move on in his life. As he holds on to the past, Holden's process of growing up becomes stunted. He calls out to Allie's memory to keep him unharmed not only as he walks along the streets of New York but as he wanders through his life. Unguided and uncertain, Holden never takes the time to cement exactly what he wants from life and as a result becomes trapped in the limbo of adolescence.

Accompanying the discovery of smudged obscenities on the walls of his younger sister Phoebe's school, Holden begins to understand that one's loss of innocence is unstoppable. He thinks of how all the children at the school would see the graffiti and, being young and innocent, not know what it meant. The thought drives him "damn near crazy" (260). Holden finds the fact that the message was written in a school for young children disturbing, wishing it were possible that Phoebe and her friends could exist untainted by such crude messages. In Holden's eyes, younger children like Phoebe represent everything that is real and pure about life, finding solace in visiting Phoebe in earlier chapters. He hates the thought that their innocence will inevitably disappear one day. After seeing a few more items of graffiti, Holden comments that "if you had a million years to do it in, you couldn't rub out even half the "F–k you" signs in the world. It's impossible" (262). Holden finally has an epiphany – he realizes that this loss of innocence is unstoppable. Society is too corrupt for there to exist a utopian, *immaculate* sanctuary free from all things foul. Though Holden spends the entire book running away from "phoniness," achieving this feat proves impossible. The reason why he notices such repulsive qualities so often is due to his age, yet he chooses to hold on to his bitterness and refuses to acknowledge this as merely a bump in the road as he grows up.

As the book draws to a close, Holden watches Phoebe ride the carrousel in Central Park and reflects on how he wishes that life could remain unchanged. When Holden hears music coming from the carrousel, he immediately recognizes the song and observes, "That's one nice thing about carrousels, they always play the same songs" (272). Like the carrousel, Holden wishes that his own life could always play the same song. His obsession with the state of things remaining untouched arises numerous times throughout the book, such as when Holden reminisces about visiting the Museum of Natural History, reveling in the way that "everything always stayed right where it was" (157) in the exhibits. This fascination could be linked to the repercussions of Allie's death on Holden. He longs for his life to return to the way it was before Allie passed, yearning for a life unaffected by such a horrific turn of events. Holden encourages Phoebe to take a ride on the carrousel, but when she asks him if he wants to come ride with her, he responds, "'No, I'll just watch ya. I think I'll just watch'" (274). Alongside other parents watching their own children, Holden stands in the pouring rain as Phoebe rides the carrousel and is moved to tears, a scene symbolizing Holden discovering closure at the end of the book. The carrousel itself is a motif, representing childhood, a stage of life that Holden finally realizes he has outgrown. He watches Phoebe on her carrousel journey as she tries to grab the gold ring, musing that "the thing with kids is, if they want to grab for the gold ring you have to let them do it, and not say anything. If they fall off, they fall off, but it's bad if you say anything to them" (273-274). For a character who consistently demonstrates irresponsibility and immaturity, Holden speaks surprisingly similar to a parent who realizes that they need to allow their children to attempt to achieve their goals independently, no matter if they succeed or fail. Holden observes Phoebe from a distance, similar to how he relates to his own childhood – literally detached, yet nostalgic. Though up to this point Holden has always remained figuratively stuck in the past, it is at this point that he understands the time has come for him to move on to another stage of his life.

Despite the fact that Holden's problems are never directly solved within the pages of the book, he still manages to gain enough closure so that the book can draw to a satisfying close. The pieces of his life are still far from reassembled; instead, Holden picks up the pieces to create a new beginning. The events of the book linger in the past, and for once, Holden seems ready to leave this behind. Holden's last words in the book indicate that his personality has not completely taken a turn for the introspective, though: "Don't ever tell anybody anything. If you do, you start missing everybody" (277).

NATIONAL BESTSELLER

INTO THE WILD

In April 1992 a young man from a well-to-do family hitchhiked to Alaska and walked alone into the wilderness north of Mt. McKinley. His name was Christopher Johnson McCandless. He had given $25,000 in savings to charity, abandoned his car and most of his possessions, burned all the cash in his wallet, and invented a new life for himself. Four months later, his decomposed body was found by a moose hunter...

JON KRAKAUER

Krakauer on McCandless: Into the Enigma

Published by Booklore

"If this adventure proves fatal and you don't ever hear from me again, I want you to know you're a great man. I now walk into the wild" (3). These words, handwritten on a postcard, marked the beginning of Christopher McCandless's fatal journey into the Alaskan interior. A college-educated twenty-four year old with a penchant for the writings of Thoreau and Tolstoy, McCandless's story of survival is one that caught widespread public attention in 1992. Deciding to run a cover story on the boy's death, Outside Magazine hired a writer named Jon Krakauer to investigate McCandless. Thus began Jon Krakauer's fascination with McCandless's life, driving him to pen *Into the Wild*. Krakauer provides a clear and detailed account of McCandless's story in an effort to help readers understand why McCandless decided to drop out of society.

An apt title, *Into the Wild* follows McCandless as he ventures straight into the wild. After graduating from Emory University, McCandless donated the contents of his savings account to OXFAM and drove to the western United States, where he strove to live off the land. Motivated by his literary idol Jack London, McCandless decided to isolate himself from the modern world as he sought personal depth and meaning. Krakauer's account explains the events of McCandless's journey thoroughly, describing how McCandless was able to survive. Deeper, though, it elaborates on who Chris McCandless was and how he thought, allowing the audience to understand him and his actions to a greater depth. At the beginning of each chapter, Krakauer includes literary quotations pertaining to McCandless's views of nature, occasionally citing quotes that McCandless had underlined in his copies of these books. One such quote, from Paul Shepard, declares that in the wild "the leaders of the great religions have sought the therapeutic and spiritual values of retreat, not to escape but to find reality" (25). *Into the Wild* is an account of McCandless's quest for such understanding.

Krakauer crafts *Into the Wild* in a straightforward style, attempting to objectively present the events of McCandless's final days. His language is concise and easily understood, making his writing accessible to readers as Krakauer runs through the facts of McCandless's story. While many biographers opt to create imaginary, though likely, scenes and events in order to make the account read more like a narrative, Krakauer instead chooses a journalistic approach to his writing. For the majority of the book, he employs an informative tone, using easily comprehensible language and logical analysis in order to make McCandless's story as clear as possible. He builds a body of evidence to support all of his claims, whether it is deep research to clarify any uncertainties or a selection from McCandless's own journal. Near the end of the book, for example, Krakauer explores a few theories surrounding McCandless's final fatal mistake. He remarks that "from all the available evidence, there seemed to be little doubt that McCandless – rash and incautious by nature – had committed a careless blunder" (192) by deciding to eat the poisonous roots of a sweet pea. However, Krakauer became increasingly dissatisfied with this theory, since there was solid evidence from McCandless's records that he had safely eaten wild potato roots without confusing them with sweet pea roots. After some investigation, including the collection of sample plants, lab analysis, and reading veterinary literature, Krakauer finally concluded that McCandless was "probably killed instead by the mold that had been growing on [wild potato] seeds" (194). Through extensive research such as this, Krakauer builds ethos and presents a reliable, logical conclusion. He acknowledges counterarguments but elaborates with just enough detail to disprove them, making his arguments all the more persuasive. Since some aspects of McCandless's final weeks will remain a mystery long into the future, this type of in-depth research proves extraordinarily helpful in filling in gaps with the most likely scenarios.

Krakauer's prose features many direct quotations from those closest to McCandless, including his immediate family and people he met while on the road. Though McCandless made a distinct effort to keep those he met at an arm's length, the quotes Krakauer chooses to include make it clear that this could be difficult for his acquaintances to accept. Particularly moving is Krakauer's passage regarding McCandless's decision to leave Ronald Franz, an elderly man whom he had met in Southern California. While McCandless felt the need to "[evade] the threat of human intimacy, of friendship, and all the messy emotional baggage that comes with it" (55), Franz felt a very strong emotional attachment to him. "'Even when he was sleeping, I was happy just knowing he was there'" (55), Franz revealed in an interview with Krakauer, even sharing that he felt strongly enough to ask McCandless if he could adopt him as a grandson. McCandless, who felt "uncomfortable with the request," decided to "dodge the question" (55) before leaving. Emotional accounts such as this convey notable elements of McCandless's psyche. Though he made a positive impact on most people he met during his travels, McCandless was never comfortable with these connections, using his solitary travels as a means of distancing himself from these people. His strong inclinations towards solitude and disillusionment with connections are exposed through testimony from his acquaintances.

Although Krakauer maintains a significant distance from the material for most of the book, during the second half he incorporates some emotion into the story to develop key themes and ideas. Earlier in the book, in fact, in the foreword, Krakauer admits that "a dispassionate rendering of the tragedy [would be] impossible" (2) for him to write. Krakauer recalls his own experiences climbing a mountain in Alaska, in the hope that drawing a parallel would "shed an oblique light on the enigma of Chris McCandless" (2). He describes climbing to the summit of the Devils Thumb, a terrifying journey that could have ended in a death similar to McCandless's. The fact that Krakauer survived, he writes, was "largely a matter of chance" (155). In his account, he emphasizes the danger of the climb just as much as his perception of that danger. In his twenties at the time, Krakauer felt that death was "largely outside [his] conceptual grasp" (145), and his long-time obsession with reaching the summit overrode any potential fatal consequences. McCandless was very much the same, so blinded by his romanticized idea of the natural world that he chose to face death head-on. Krakauer admits that he, like McCandless, was naïve in his idealism about the natural world, but because of his obsession with climbing the Devils Thumb, "life thrummed at a higher pitch" and "the world was made real" (134). Many of McCandless's critics speculate that he was suicidal, since his chances for survival seemed slim at best, but Krakauer states that he can understand McCandless's motivations. He makes a persuasive case against such critics by including this narrative, which also closes the distance between Krakauer and his audience, adding an affective side to his writing.

Krakauer has achieved something commendable through *Into the Wild*. Instead of walking away from the book with knowledge of a young man's final traipse into nature, readers close the pages of Into the Wild with a thorough knowledge of McCandless himself. What might have been a mere adventure story becomes a psychological portrait of an adventurer whom readers identify with, and possibly one day become.

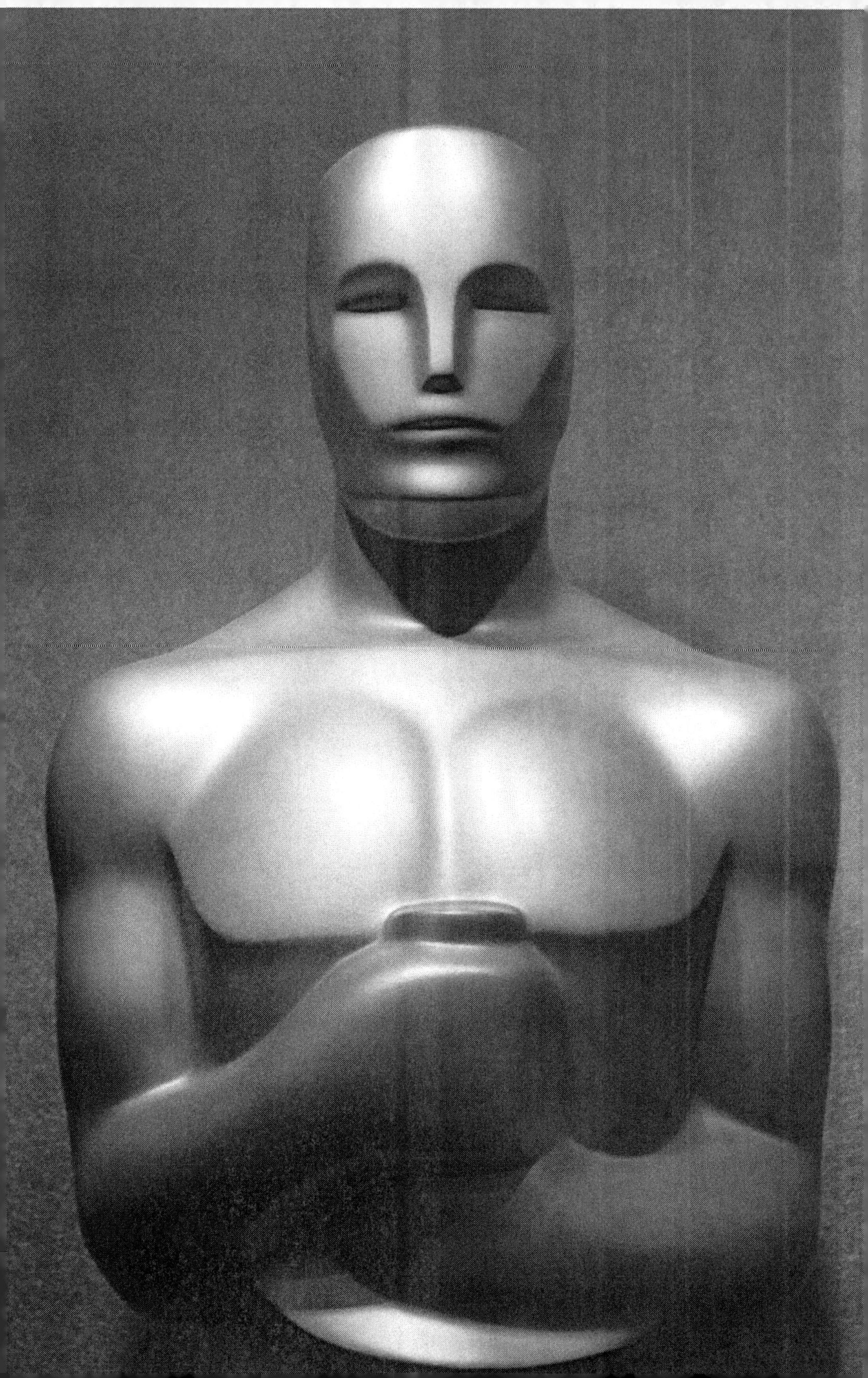

2011 Oscars

The CCHS student newspaper, The Voice, *ran two companion pieces written before and after the 2011 Oscars.*

SparkNotes: Oscar Nominations

Awards season continues to honor 2010's standout works of art with the Oscars on Sunday, February 27. Whether one believes that the Academy spotlights quality films with true artistic value or just hands out awards on the basis of popularity, there is no doubt that the ceremony will give viewers much to talk about. The A&E department of The Voice would like to guide readers through the nominations and break down some of the most talked-about categories before the nominees hit the red carpet.

BEST PICTURE

Nominees: *Black Swan, The Fighter, Inception, The Kids Are All Right, The King's Speech, 127 Hours, The Social Network, Toy Story 3,* and *Winter's Bone*

What's likely to happen: The predictable take: this competition is between *The King's Speech* and *The Social Network*, darlings of the Golden Globes. However, the Academy occasionally chooses an unexpected winner – take *Crash*'s win in 2005 as an example – so we may see a film like *127 Hours* or *The Kids Are All Right* taking away the trophy. Realistically, films like *Inception* or *Toy Story 3* probably would not have made it onto the ballot if there were still a five-nominee limit, despite how well-made they were. This category is always a bit up in the air and difficult to predict.

Who should win: *The Social Network*

89

ACTOR IN A LEADING ROLE

Nominees: Javier Bardem – *Biutiful*, Jeff Bridges – *True Grit*, Jesse Eisenberg – *The Social Network*, Colin Firth – *The King's Speech*, James Franco – *127 Hours*

What's likely to happen: Again, another category that's difficult to call. Jeff Bridges and Colin Firth are both veterans, James Franco is well-respected and well-established, and Jesse Eisenberg was one of the most talked-about new talents of 2010. He could be the youngest winner of the Oscar (and rightly so – his portrayal of the Facebook creator Mark Zuckerberg is socially uncomfortable yet beautiful and reptilian). Colin Firth is certainly a notable contender, but I have a feeling the Academy may choose to spotlight James Franco for his role trapped behind a boulder in *127 Hours*.

Who should win: Jesse Eisenberg – *The Social Network* (Close readers might be sensing a pattern developing)

ACTRESS IN A LEADING ROLE

Nominees: Annette Bening – *The Kids Are All Right*, Nicole Kidman – *Rabbit Hole*, Jennifer Lawrence – *Winter's Bone*, Natalie Portman – *Black Swan*, Michelle Williams – *Blue Valentine*

What's likely to happen: Natalie Portman wins. They don't even need to open the envelope.

Who should win: Natalie Portman – *Black Swan*

DIRECTING

Nominees: Darren Aronofsky – *Black Swan*, David O. Russell – *The Fighter*, Tom Hooper – *The King's Speech*, David Fincher – *The Social Network*, Joel Coen and Ethan Coen – *True Grit*

What's likely to happen: David Fincher and Darren Aronofsky seem to be the frontrunners here. Since this is a more obscure category, though, the Academy might stray from the obvious and choose Tom Hooper for *The King's Speech* for directing such a phenomenal cast.

Who should win: Christopher Nolan – *Inception* (Wait, he's not nominated? Oh…)

MUSIC (ORIGINAL SCORE)

Nominees: John Powell - *How to Train Your Dragon*, Hans Zimmer - *Inception*, Alexandre Desplat - *The King's Speech*, A.R. Rahman - *127 Hours*, Trent Reznor and Atticus Ross - *The Social Network*

What's likely to happen: Trent Reznor of electronic rock band Nine Inch Nails has already been honored by the Golden Globes for branching out into scoring films, but this won't stop the Academy from giving him the Oscar. Hans Zimmer is, unfortunately, too obvious a choice, and the other composers are filler nominations. Expect Trent and Atticus to take this one home.

Who should win: Hans Zimmer - *Inception*

Stay tuned for the results!

The King's Sweep: Brits Clean Up at 2011 Oscars

There were few surprises at the 83rd annual Academy Awards on Sunday, February 27 as The King's Speech cast its shadow over the major award categories. In fact, there were very few upsets whatsoever over the course of the ceremony. Yes, Natalie Portman won Best Actress. Yes, Colin Firth won Best Actor. And oh yes, *Toy Story 3* won Best Animated Film. Which begs the question: were the Oscars worth watching when viewers already had accurate results written on their prediction scorecards?

The Oscars, already notorious for tediously dragging on and on into the night, lack the party atmosphere of the Golden Globes. Rather than the freedom and looseness of tables (and, of course, alcohol), the actors are confined to seats in the Kodak Theatre. At first, it seemed that hosts James Franco and Anne Hathaway might have been able to bring the same type of energy to the ceremony that Billy Crystal would, had he been able to host the show again. The Oscars kicked off with a hilarious video clip in which Franco and Hathaway attempted to perform inception on Alec Baldwin. However, it seemed that they hit their stride too early. The ceremony still felt about eight hours long rather than three and a half. While comedians are certainly capable of making small quips between awards to pass the time, a preoccupied Franco appeared to be pondering his imminent PhD or the R.E.M. video he's slated to direct.

Awards were not divided evenly between the two major contenders for best picture, *The Social Network* and *The King's Speech*. While *The Social Network* earned some minor – and well-deserved – awards, including Best Original Score and Best Adapted Screenplay, *The King's Speech* still won Best Director, Best Actor, and Best Picture.

David Fincher's loss of Best Director to *Speech*'s Tom Hooper was perhaps the most surprising win, though the award only added to the overwhelming trend of *The King's Speech*. "I am just stunned that David Fincher didn't win, just absolutely stunned," commented Kevin Spacey, executive producer of *The Social Network*, perhaps with a slight bias toward his own production. (NB: The author of this article happens to share this slight bias, in case readers are wondering.) Along with some colorful language, Spacey added, "This just proves it is all about campaigning and nothing else. It's just a popularity contest."

Indeed, *The King's Speech* did campaign heavily throughout awards season, effectively generating enough Oscar hype after its December 2010 release. *The Social Network*, released in October 2010, did not employ the same strategy, which could explain its loss of momentum. *The Fighter* also made good use of pre-Oscars promotion, and it showed – the film collected both Best Supporting Actor and Best Supporting Actress for Christian Bale and Melissa Leo. So, is Spacey right? Is the ceremony just a popularity contest, and is promotion the only way to win? Or, do upsets exist within the realm of possibility, helping films like 2005's *Crash* win best picture?

Stay tuned until the 2012 Oscars…

RADIOHEAD
THE KING OF LIMBS

Radiohead:
The King of Limbs and Future Branches
Published by CCHS student newspaper The Voice

The ultimate Valentine's Day surprise awaited all Radiohead fans this past February 14. On the homepage of the band's website appeared an abstract drawing of a tree creature, along with the bold, succinct message "THANK YOU FOR WAITING." Months of anticipation and speculation had led to this JPEG. An excited click on the image opened up thekingoflimbs.com, which informed ecstatic music fans that "The new Radiohead record, *The King of Limbs,* is through here."

This piece of information led to various levels of hysteria in front of the computer screen. A few short clicks revealed that a digital download of the album would be available on February 19 – five short days later. Unsurprisingly, this news spread like wildfire throughout the music universe. Although front man Thom Yorke was certainly out and about in 2010, embarking on a solo tour across the US with a few one-off shows in Europe, news about the full band's recording process was relatively scarce (That is, apart from one notorious June 2010 radio interview with guitarist/self-proclaimed optimist Ed O'Brien, who reported that Radiohead would release the new album "in a matter of weeks." Sure…30 weeks). Rush-releasing *The King of Limbs* was the correct response to such build-up. Luckily, O'Brien managed to redeem himself by means of a February 18 post on the Radiohead website: "It's Friday…It's almost the weekend…It's a full moon… You can download *The King of Limbs* now if you so wish! Thank you good

95

people for waiting…Have a nice weekend…" Always so courteous, those English boys, especially when they release an album a day early.

Instead of a pay-what-you-want scheme, which the band employed for the release of its previous record, In Rainbows, fans need to pay set prices to obtain *The King of Limbs*. A digital download is as inexpensive as $9.00, while a deluxe "Newspaper Album" costs $48.00. The deluxe version includes vinyl records, a CD, a digital download, and "many large sheets of artwork, 625 tiny pieces of artwork, and a full-color piece of oxo-degradable plastic to hold it all together." The physical components of the deluxe version ship on Monday, May 9.

As one of the most innovative acts in the music industry, Radiohead constantly re-develops its sound and experiments while still keeping a firm grip on cohesion. The new record is no exception to this principle. Its multi-layered, intricate sounds reward repeat listens and active listener participation. Album opener *Bloom*'s syncopated beats, piano loops, and Colin Greenwood's excellent bass parts lull listeners into a trance that album closer *Separator* eventually casts away as Thom Yorke croons, "Wake me up." Many will recognize the accessible *Lotus Flower* due to its now infamous video, featuring Yorke performing a signature interpretive dance to the song. While most fans enjoyed the album, many complained about its length – a mere eight songs and 38 minutes, the shortest release from Radiohead yet.

Or is it?

As always with Radiohead fans, conspiracy abounds. Many are theorizing that a follow-up to the album will be released soon. Certain songs Yorke debuted on his solo tour, such as *The Present Tense*, were not included on the album, and a few sources close to the band have hinted that they are not on the tracklisting for *The King of Limbs* "yet." The meaning of the name "Newspaper Album" for the deluxe version is still unclear, and fans speculate that perhaps there are multiple editions of the album as with a newspaper. For any other band, this level of hypothesizing would seem ludicrous, but this is Radiohead, arguably the most unconventional band in the music industry. Lead guitarist Jonny Greenwood has confirmed that Radiohead is "recording at the moment" but then clarified that the band has "stopped planning ahead very far, just making music and wondering where to go next and what to do." Whatever avenue the band travels down next, it is safe to say that no one will have accurately predicted it on a message board. For now, *The King of Limbs* itself will do.

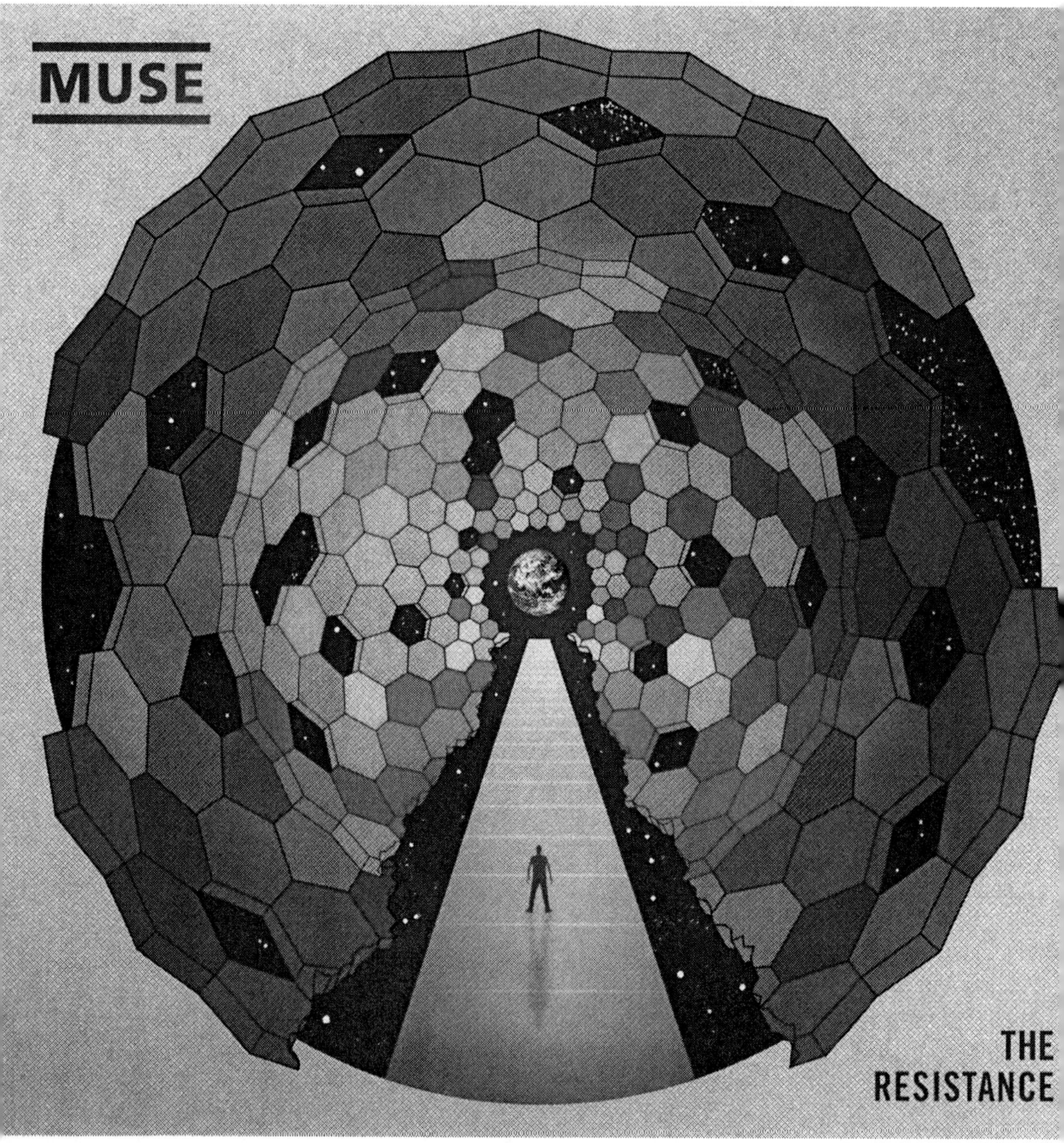
MUSE
THE
RESISTANCE

The Resistance by Muse: CD Review

Published by CCHS student newspaper The Voice

I can still remember the exact three words that sprung to mind when I finally received my first taste of the brand new Muse album, *The Resistance*, one July morning. Muse had just released the first available clip of the record to cyberspace for their die-hard fans to finally hear. The months of anticipation had mounted and the first moment of truth had arrived. I pressed play and the initial impression came rushing toward me in the form of three words: This is insane.

The song was titled "United States of Eurasia (+ Collateral Damage)," and Muse are arguably the only band on the face of the planet that would dare to write such a song. With some deceptively mellow piano at the forefront, the song soon explodes into stacked Freddie Mercury harmonies complete with string arrangements reminiscent of "Live and Let Die" before reaching its denouement in the form of a Chopin nocturne. Oh, and the lyrics are inspired by a book called *The Grand Chessboard: American Primacy and its Geostrategic Imperatives*. Even for a band touted as one of the most over-the-top and experimental of the new millennium, the song pushes the envelope. Yet, somehow it manages to work.

The Resistance in full is a similar experience: Unashamedly over-the-top but still able to hold its own as nothing short of a fantastic album. No two songs are alike, and the album explores all dusty corners of the musical spectrum. The first track and first single, "Uprising," kicks off with Chris Wolstenholme's trademark thick bass and evolves into a guitar-driven battle cry. The anthemic vocals of "They will not control us" at the song's chorus set the tone for the rest of the album. The song cuts for the ethereal synths of the title track, "Resistance," to begin to build, a light piano melody coasting over the airy environment. The tone shifts from aggressive to introspective musically and lyrically, already an indication of just how much musical ground The Resistance covers.

Another highlight is "Undisclosed Desires," a cut destined to be a single with its immensely catchy pop sensibility. It is the band-described "anti-Muse song" – Dom Howard's drum beats are abandoned for electronic drum machines, Chris Wolstenholme revives slap bass from a multiple-decade coma, and guitar and piano parts are swapped for string samples layered above a backdrop of Depeche Mode-esque synths. Though the song appears to have nothing going for it, "Undisclosed" is unique and easily one of the album's best.

The cut "Unnatural Selection" brings back memories of Muse's early days, where manic, heavy riffs were the largest concern. The song is an epic; a sizeable dose of hard rock goodness that is sure to be seven minutes of pure gold whenever the band plays it live.

Though some songs lack total immediacy and impact, primarily the power ballad of sorts "Guiding Light," *The Resistance* is a musical odyssey, rising and falling at the appropriate times. It culminates in the only way such a full-blown, massive album ever could: with a three-part symphony following a loose apocalyptic narrative, of course. "Exogenesis" for example is a cinematic world of its own. The swirling string arrangements and piano parts sound like they could find their home on any classical music station, while the drum and bass in the background maintain the piece's status as a prog-rock opus. A subconscious division between the first eight songs, the standalone "album tracks" so to speak, and "Exogenesis" is almost inevitable. A perfect capper to such an album, the symphony is honestly incredible enough that it could stand alone as an EP.

Vocalist, guitarist, pianist, and general mastermind behind all things Muse Matt Bellamy puts it this way: *The Resistance* has "got everything. It's the summation of every type of music we've ever explored." In the hands of any other band, such an undertaking would easily have hurtled off the freeway and crashed headfirst into a tree but Muse successfully tie together all loose ends while keeping the ever-abundant excess under control. The album's brilliance cannot be ignored – in that particular case, resistance is futile.

Grade: A

READING CLASSICS

ERNEST HEMINGWAY

The Old Man and the Sea

CIDEB

Santiago as the Hemingway Code Hero: A Study in Grace Under Pressure

Published by Teen Ink

The prolific author Ernest Hemingway once defined courage as "grace under pressure." This best describes a specific breed of protagonists known as the Hemingway Code Hero. A Hemingway Code Hero is a character who must conduct his life with a certain code of living when faced with the prospect of his own mortality. The qualities of courage, humility, and dignity in the face of defeat define a Hemingway hero. These same qualities also define Santiago, the main character of Hemingway's novella *The Old Man and the Sea*. Barely a shell of a man, living in poverty and without catching a single fish for eighty-four days, Santiago sets out to hook a massive marlin in order to support himself and his noticeable scarcities. The voyage tests Santiago's physical and emotional strength – he tightly clenches his morals and his values in the face of danger so as to persevere through the epic struggle. As a Hemingway Code Hero, Santiago proves time and time again throughout the novella that external obstacles are not as important as one's internal courage and dignity when it ultimately comes to one's survival.

A vital component of the old man's personality that proves crucial to his survival is his youthful energy and spirit. From the exterior, Santiago does not appear to be heroic. Hemingway introduces him as "an old man who fished alone in a skiff in the Gulf Stream and he had gone eighty-four days now without taking a fish" (9). A wiry old man with "deep-creased scars [on his hands] from handling heavy fish on the cords" (10), at first glance, Santiago seems to be quite fragile and far from the ideal, picturesque hero. However, his appearance is the only area in which Santiago has lost his youth, as "everything about him was old except his eyes and they were the same color as the sea and were cheerful and undefeated" (10). This single line allows readers to glimpse Santiago's major heroic qualities. While his body may seem to be broken and defeated, his eyes are resilient and triumphant, much like his soul. Without this spirit, Santiago would lack the energy to be persistent in the conflict with the marlin. While the handicap of his aging body becomes more and more apparent as the story progresses, what with his fading strength and injured palms, Santiago's inner strength prevails and provokes him to "fight until [he] die[s]" (115).

While the definition of a Hemingway Code Hero differs greatly from that of a stereotypical "hero," a common trait that all heroes share is bravery. Throughout the struggle with the marlin, Santiago continually displays courage and fortitude in the face of pain and suffering. For instance, Santiago's fishing line cuts deeply into his hand as he attempts to reel in the marlin. Santiago "felt the line carefully with his right hand and noticed his hand was bleeding" (55-56). Despite the tremendous physical pain, Santiago faces his suffering valiantly. Hemingway Code Heroes maintain dignity in the midst of suffering and defeat, so the unspoken code requires Santiago to proceed further into the struggle. Santiago "was comfortable but suffering, although he did not admit the suffering at all" (64) – the response an ideal Code Hero would have to a situation such as this. Without such strength, the motivation to succeed and press on until the end of the fight would deplete with the onset of any major hindrance. One would find it impossible to accomplish anything with willpower as weak as this. Santiago later comments that "pain does not matter to a man" (84) as he examines his injured right hand, the mentality a true Hemingway Code Hero possesses.

Throughout the story, Santiago exhibits the value and worth of humility in a Code Hero. Early on in the story, Hemingway reveals that Santiago "was too simple to wonder when he had attained humility. But he knew he had attained it and he knew it was not disgraceful and it carried no loss of true pride" (13-14). While Santiago takes pride in his emotional strength in that he constantly refuses to admit defeat (as his moral code dictates), he does not possess foolish pride in the sense of rank. Santiago does not believe he is better than anyone else, and realizes the importance of humility in life. His tremendous humility becomes even more visible during his battle with the marlin. Santiago notes that he and the fish have different strengths – Santiago carries the gift of human intelligence, yet the marlin is "more noble and able" (63). He struggles with the question of whether or not the fish is worthy of being killed and eaten, deciding "there is no one worthy of eating him from the manner of his behavior and his great dignity" (75). Santiago does not regard himself as any better off than the fish; rather, he thinks of the marlin as an admirable opponent, a "brother" (59). Yet, he never loses sight of the true fight – he is always focused on the task at hand (catching the marlin) and perseveres, following the code in order to accomplish what he intended to. Santiago's humility keeps him grounded, allowing him to remain morally well-rounded as he fights to reel in the marlin.

Santiago's numerous challenges and triumph over adversity appear continually throughout the work. Santiago's seeming lack of physical strength almost convinces him he cannot continue, however, Santiago reminds himself that "man is not made for defeat…a man can be destroyed but not defeated" (103). This statement reflects the true sentiment of the Hemingway Code Hero – never backing down in the midst of defeat while ensuring that one's moral code remains intact. The heroic nature of Santiago comes alive when he seems to be most defeated. While he may appear unsuccessful externally as the novella draws to a close, his internal dignity never wavers. He constantly stays true to his code in the face of adversity – in the face of death he reaffirms his life and worthiness in the universe. Santiago illuminates the basic essence of the Hemingway Code Hero, the knowledge that triumph is associated with internal strength and dignity in the center of a chaotic, suffering world.

ARCADE FIRE

The Suburbs by Arcade Fire: CD Review

Published by CCHS student newspaper The Voice

As someone who was getting more and more bored by new album releases that sounded identical to one another, I was not expecting much from an album with the vague and uninteresting title *The Suburbs*. Luckily, I was pleasantly surprised that this album, the new Arcade Fire album, had the power to completely restore my faith in new music. From the first chord of the first track, *The Suburbs* transports listeners into its own world. The lyrical content is instantly relatable: not quite a concept album, but a loose narrative that anyone from suburbia can understand. An entire album about growing up in the suburbs appears to be dry subject matter for a rock record, but events never stand still. The "suburban wars" among different cliques of kids growing up and apart (highlighted in the track "Suburban War" - "Now the music divides us into tribes/You grew your hair, so I grew mine") are constantly discussed amidst an atmospheric instrumental backdrop.

At the same time, the stagnant nature of suburban life is also captured perfectly. The kids in the suburbs all dream of one day escaping their town, but then as they mature, they realize the impracticalities of their dreams. When they drive away from their hometown at night in "Half Light II (No Celebration)," their longing for adventure and youthful spirit is harshly grounded in reality ("When we watched the markets crash, the promises we made were torn"). The idleness of wasting time as teenagers comes up in the stunning "Wasted Hours," as teenagers are not quite sure what to do with free time, but are always "staring out the window," wanting something more from life but still too young to escape the monotony of a small town.

Musically, Arcade Fire creates a suitable soundscape to fit the lyrics. There is no enormous sing-along anthem like "Wake Up," but then again, that would not make much sense in this context. The instrumentation of the first track, "The Suburbs," sets the tone for the entire album – a simple guitar chord progression with soft piano and a constant, straight drumbeat. The music is not intended to be intrusive or take over the song, but it provides just the right amount of mood. From the chugging power chords of obvious future single "Month of May" to the danceable percussion of the synth-based epic "Sprawl II (Mountains Beyond Mountains)," the album covers enough musical ground to stay diverse and interesting while still remaining cohesive. The album is intended to be listened to from start to finish, as it feels more like one distinct musical thought with sixteen movements rather than a collection of sixteen unrelated songs. This is a refreshing change for a rock album, as the album format seems to have been getting lost in the fog recently.

The final song on the album, "The Suburbs (Continued)," begins with the lyric, "If I could have it back/All the time that we wasted/I'd only waste it again." The same is true of listening to the album, though it hardly feels like wasted time. This is a dynamic drive through suburban life and arguably the best album of 2010 thus far.

Grade: A

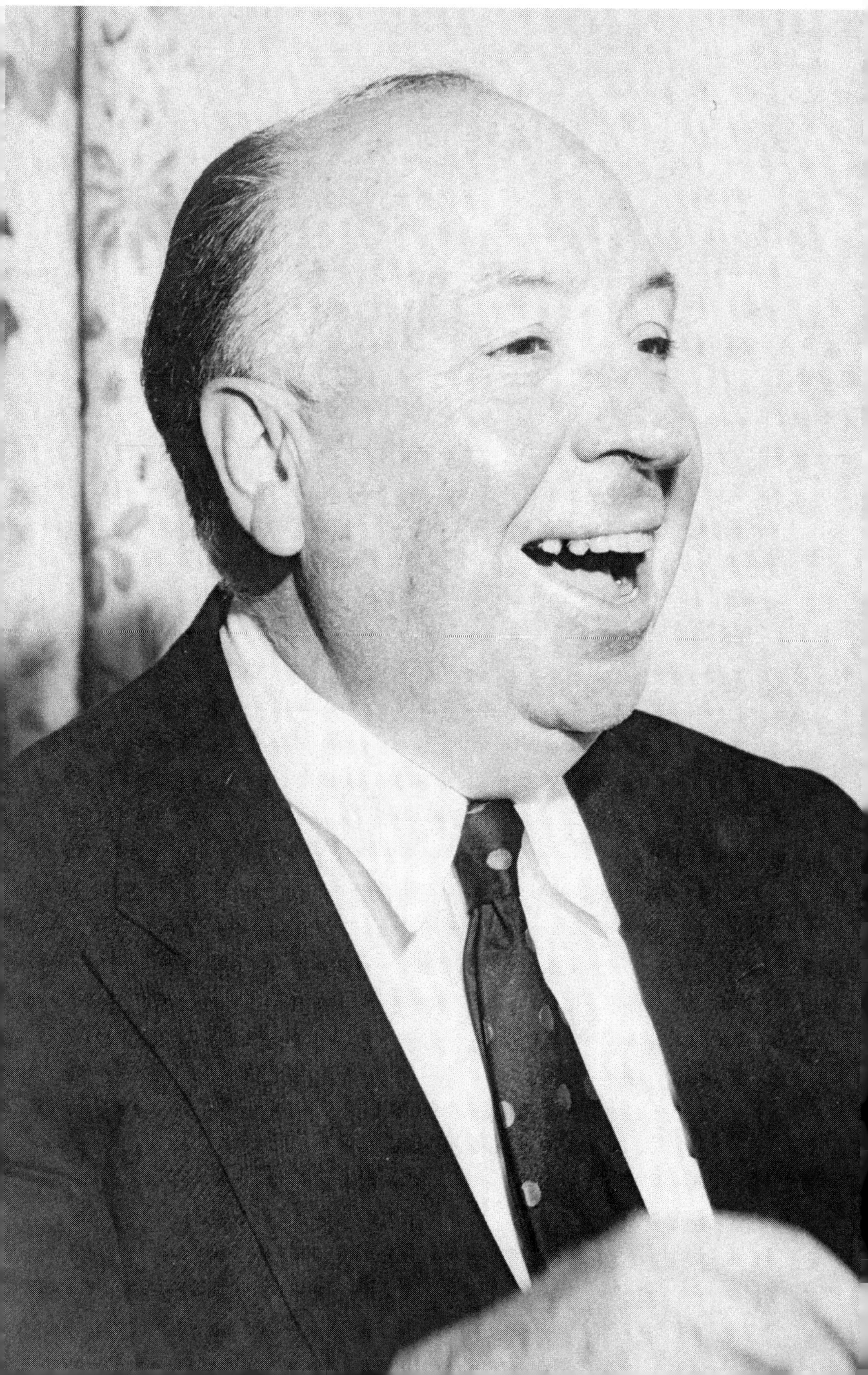

Shine a Light: Alfred Hitchcock's Usage of Lighting in Film

Published by Teen Ink

Seemingly innocuous details often make a significant difference in film. A cinematic technique such as lighting may not be the most immediately noticeable aspect of a sequence of film, but it can play an integral role in enhancing a movie's overall imagery. One director who took full advantage of this technique was Alfred Hitchcock. Throughout his career, he paid full attention to lighting details and ensured that each shot carried significant creative weight.

In the bank robbing sequence from "Marnie," the lighting and shadows add to the emotional tension of the scene. Before the robbery, Marnie hides in a bathroom stall to wait for the building to empty out. Her head is positioned in the bottom right corner of the lengthy shot, the most vulnerable area of the screen, conveying both the risk involved with her plan and the notion that anything could go wrong at any particular moment. Marine's face is also partially in the shadows, representing the shady nature of her character and serving to keep her hidden more completely. Hitchcock uses other elements, such as sound, to enhance the sequence. As Marnie listens to see if everyone has finally left, the audience finds themselves listening to see if they, too, feel that it is safe for Marnie to leave the stall. Accompanying this sound is the shadow of the bathroom door opening and closing, which is visible against the wall in the upper left hand corner. This is an interesting yet uncertain way of showing people filing out of the bathroom and, subsequently, the building. The audience is emotionally engaged throughout the scene, which is an achievement considering how uninteresting a shot of a woman's face could be.

The lighting in the film "Strangers on a Train" symbolically indicates the true nature of the characters. During the opening scene where Bruno and Guy are talking on the train, Bruno sits so that the shadow of the compartment's venetian blinds hits his face directly. The shadows are horizontal and resemble the bars of a jail cell. In contrast, no shadows darken Guy's face. Even before ten minutes of the film have passed, the lighting sends a subliminal message that Bruno's character is the one who is not meant to be trusted. Later on in the film, once Bruno has killed Guy's wife, another display of symbolic shadows can be observed. Bruno stands across the street from Guy's house, far enough into the shadows so that his face is not visible. He calls Guy over to tell him the news, and Guy leaves the entrance of his brightly lit apartment to speak with Bruno. Guy stands in the light while they speak to separate himself from Bruno's plan, but once the police arrive at Guy's house to inform him of the murder, Guy also hides in the shadows with Bruno. Guy was aware of Bruno's plan, and his move into the shadows symbolizes this awareness. Once Guy decides he wants nothing to do with Bruno, he storms out of the shadows and back into his home, representing his decision to oppose Bruno for the remainder of the movie.

In "Vertigo," however, Hitchcock reaches the symbolic apex of film lighting. Throughout the movie, the color green symbolizes mystery. When Johnny initially pursued Madeline by car, she drove a green car representing the mysterious circumstances surrounding her situation and identity. Even after Madeline has seemingly committed suicide, Johnny first spots Judy wearing a green dress, indicating that Judy herself may be an extension of the film's mystery. In Judy's hotel room, however, the lighting takes on the main responsibilities of the enigmatic green motif. A green light from one of the neon signs on the street shines into Judy's room, casting an eerie green glow. Hitchcock uses this green light in a few significant ways apart from straight-ahead lighting. When Judy first appears dressed similar to Madeline, the green light makes her appear to be glowing. She comes across Johnny as an apparition of Madeline, but viewers know that the green color indicates the secrets of her identity. The green light also highlights Judy's silhouette, further reinforcing her status as Madeline reincarnated in Johnny's eyes. In truth, Judy was impersonating Madeline, but Johnny was oblivious of this fact. The usage of green lighting intensifies Johnny's fascination with the uncanny similarities between Madeline and Judy.

Not many would immediately point to lighting as an integral medium of expressing a film's themes, but Hitchcock brought this technique to the foreground. It is a powerful way of conveying mood, but Hitchcock understood its less obvious extensions, which made his work more powerful. The depth of the less noticeable made Hitchcock films masterpieces, securing them a permanent spot in the history of film.

HISTORY and POLITICAL AFFAIRS

CLEOPATRA

A LIFE

STACY SCHIFF
WINNER OF THE PULITZER PRIZE

Demystifying a Legend: Reviewing Stacy Schiff's *Cleopatra*

Published by Booklore

AUTHOR'S THESIS:

Although Cleopatra is one of the most famous figures of the ancient world, most modern knowledge about her has been shaped by myths and fantasy. Because of this, writing Cleopatra's biography becomes multiple times more difficult – not only are concrete sources very scarce, the few sources that do remain are "often overblown [by mythical embellishment]… the point was to dazzle" (7). Through her book, *Cleopatra: A Life*, Stacy Schiff attempts to "peel away the encrusted myth and the hoary propaganda" (7) to write a biography of Cleopatra that is characterized by historical accuracy. An additional objective complemented this attempt at total accuracy, as Schiff wanted to "thread through the book" that "history comes down to us as propaganda and hearsay…how history gets written is as important as what it tells us" (Schiff, *Barnes and Noble Review*). Most sources "relied to a great extent on memory" and produced "overblown" (7) accounts. Roman historians would have been affected by Octavian's negative presentation of Cleopatra to the Roman people, as he discussed her in "hyperbolized" (5) terms in order to magnify the glory of her defeat. Even Plutarch, a Greek historian who would have escaped Roman bias, was writing about Cleopatra nearly eight decades after her death, relying on oral history from his grandfather's generation. He was also prone to embellishing major details, as he was "as taken with her as was anyone in her lifetime" (Pitz). Although the reliability of these sources was discouraging, Schiff recognized these were the only sources in existence. Thus, writing the book required not only deep research, but judgment and deduction to clarify the facts.

As she noted about her sources, Schiff understood that it would be impossible for her to write this biography without some of her own personal bias seeping in. As a woman with a 21st century perspective, Schiff felt "much more inclined to view [Cleopatra] as a three-dimensional woman" (Schiff, *Publishers Weekly*). While wading through research, Schiff discovered a consistent focus on Cleopatra's personal life rather than her political accomplishments. As she says in the final chapter of her book, "We will remember that Cleopatra slept with Julius Caesar and Mark Antony long after we have forgotten what she accomplished in doing so" (299). In her book, Schiff focuses on Cleopatra's ability to sustain her own country's strength, fostering Egypt's economic prosperity and intellectual growth. She also suggests that Cleopatra was in tune with the political advantages of securing Rome as an ally – she knew that the financially suffering republic would be reliant on the wealth of Egypt for their military, and in return, she would gain protection from one of the Mediterranean's strongest civilizations. Schiff acknowledges that Cleopatra was witty, strategic, and intellectual, but avoids painting her as a manipulative seductress. In striving for truth, Schiff strips away the myth surrounding Cleopatra's persona. Although many details will remain unknown forever, *Cleopatra: A Life* demystifies the legend and presents a tangible account of cloudy history.

SUMMARY:

Schiff follows Cleopatra's life chronologically, from her childhood to the questionable circumstances surrounding her death. Since "virtually nothing" (27) is known about Cleopatra's childhood, Schiff examines her likely education as a springboard for understanding her formative years. Cleopatra would have been well-versed in the art of rhetoric, clearly learning to "marshal her thoughts precisely, express them artistically, deliver them gracefully" (31), informing her notoriously captivating manner of speaking. Also crucial is Cleopatra's knowledge of the spoken Egyptian language, making her the first member of the Ptolemy dynasty to be able to speak directly with her Egyptian subjects.

Cleopatra's relationship with Julius Caesar is the focal point of the book's first few chapters. Schiff suggests that the two shared similar interests – both were well-educated, both were talented orators, both were partial to extravagance. Their relationship prompted a war between Rome and Egypt, Cleopatra siding with Caesar against the king of Egypt, her own brother, Ptolemy XIII. By the end of the conflict, the Romans had forced Ptolemy to flee and Cleopatra officially became the queen of Egypt. Within two months, Cleopatra had given birth to Caesar's son, Caesarion, creating a royal lineage to secure her throne. With Egypt under control, Cleopatra followed Caesar back to Rome, where many Egyptian-influenced reforms were taking place. Caesar opened a public library, echoing the one in Alexandria, and he decided to drain marshes in central Italy in order to create more fertile farmland. Caesar's murder brought this chapter of Cleopatra's life to an abrupt end. Schiff notes that Cleopatra may have influenced Caesar's tastes for extravagance that enraged the conspirators, but it is "debatable" (128) that Cleopatra played any role in the events leading up to the end of Caesar's life. No sources comment on Cleopatra's reaction to the event - something Schiff calls "frustrating" (Schiff, Barnes and Noble Review) due to the immense cost of losing Caesar. Understanding that she could be in danger of assassination in the aftermath of Caesar's murder, Cleopatra did quickly make her way back to Egypt to foster its ongoing intellectual revival.

This Golden Age was interrupted in the year 43 B.C., which saw the onset of Egyptian agricultural crises and the return of Roman civil war to Alexandria. While Cleopatra might have "preferred to steer clear" of Roman conflicts, she also had "little choice" (157) in the matter due to her connection to Caesar. Thus, she decided to ally herself with Roman general Mark Antony in the civil war. A thirteen-year love affair soon followed, one that both recognized as politically convenient – Cleopatra needed Antony's forces to protect Egypt, and Antony needed Cleopatra's wealth to fund military campaigns in Parthia. In 32 B.C., Octavian, vying for total control of Rome, used their relationship to spark a conflict with Antony. He argued that Cleopatra had "subdued Antony" (242), and she was planning on taking over Rome as well. The Battle of Actium, in which Antony unintentionally deserted his men, led to Octavian's ascension to Roman power. As emperor, Octavian took Cleopatra prisoner after Antony committed suicide, mistakenly believing Cleopatra herself was dead. Cleopatra ultimately met her end as Octavian's prisoner, not by means of cobra venom but more likely by means of a self-administered poison drink. Her death would have been "peaceful, swift, and essentially painless" (286), marking the end of the era of the Roman Republic and the beginning of the Roman Empire. To some extent, even though it took a few centuries, her demise also represented the beginning of Egypt's years of decline.

REVIEW:

Although it might seem that a book about Cleopatra's life would primarily focus on her life in Egypt, her close ties to powerful Romans called for much reporting on the state of the Roman Republic during her lifetime. Cleopatra's visit to Caesar's Rome was a jarring transition – she left Alexandria's vivacious culture, beautiful weather, and majestic architecture for Rome's stifling, unhygienic, chaotic streets. Schiff refers to Rome's inferiority complex towards the Greeks, which came up in our class discussions this past semester. Although the Romans were quickly gaining power and leverage in the Mediterranean, they lacked Greece's high societal standards, as Greece "continued to spell culture, elegance, [and] art" (109). Rome was steadily becoming more aware of these shortcomings, and as a result, it began to reject the excesses of other cultures. Needless to say, Alexandria provided an easy target. Masking their envy of Egypt's financial stability and power, Romans would refer to the pyramids as "idle and foolish ostentations of royal wealth" (109). All Alexandrian imports were written off as either barbaric or far too decadent.

The Roman outlook on the rights of women also starkly contrasted with that of the Egyptians, making Cleopatra's life all the more difficult. In Rome, "female authority was a meaningless concept" (111), and they were expected to blend into the background. Women did not even have their own personal names, inheriting the female version of their father's name, much less any natural rights. Cleopatra, however, was accustomed to a society in which she needed to make any public appearance a city-wide spectacle. She had grown up in Egypt, the most progressive Mediterranean country, where women were able to divorce their husbands, inherit money, hold property, initiate lawsuits, and essentially remain in charge of their own lives. Instead of the all-white wardrobe of a Roman, Cleopatra sported vibrant colors and extravagant jewelry. Inconspicuousness was not one of Cleopatra's strengths.

Needless to say, it was impossible for Cleopatra to quietly assimilate into Roman society – not only was she a woman, she was "richer than any man in Rome" (112), multiplying the public scorn. The Roman outlook on Cleopatra informed the way she was portrayed throughout history, as many historians "constructed [her story] as much of male fear as of fantasy" (300).

The contrast between both civilizations greatly surprised me as I was reading the book. I never had any inkling that any country in the ancient world was as forward-thinking as Egypt in terms of feminism, which was refreshing to read about. This also added to the impact of Cleopatra's death, since legal autonomy for women disintegrated along with Alexandria's power. I was also taken aback by the way Schiff depicted Rome. I was aware that it was a few cultural steps behind the other notable Mediterranean civilizations, but I didn't realize how large the gap actually was. When Cleopatra visited Rome, the society had "only just discovered urban design" (109). Previously, the organization of the city was not planned or thought-out, and it showed. The city was "an oriental tangle of narrow, poorly ventilated streets and ceaseless, shutter-creaking commotion" (108), both squalid and unsanitary. As we discussed in class, the wealthier classes did exist, but poor Romans dominated the population without much of a middle class to balance it out. To Cleopatra, this inside look at Rome must have been just as perplexing, considering the strength of the civilization as a whole.

The book also gave an interesting view of Roman politics. In particular, Schiff described the way politicians avoided looking at the actual issues at hand. Even when Caesar was assassinated, a politically charged act, "enmity rather than issues" (148) ruled people's opinions in their assessment of that event. Schiff also addressed the self-absorbed nature of the Roman Senate. When Octavian and Antony began to clash for control of Rome, the Senators did nothing to end this conflict and prevent civil war. They decided it was "far better that the two rivals obstruct each other…than that they join forces" (145), understanding that any cooperation between the two could mean the end for their own power, their most prized possession. The Senators were correct in their thinking – when Octavian and Antony realized they needed to work together for control of Rome, they "agreed that the Senate was the main source of [political] troubles" (Lendering). They then proceeded to eliminate "nearly a third of the Senate" (153) and its supporters through proscription.

Rome's political undertakings required sufficient funding, something which proved challenging to attain. This amplified the importance of the civilization's ties to Cleopatra – although the Romans might have cast a scornful eye at the excesses of her culture, they could not deny that they depended on her for wealth. Antony especially relied on Cleopatra for money during his scuffles with Octavian for control of Rome. Antony was fixated on successfully carrying out a military campaign in Parthia, as he knew that "only an Eastern victory could once and for all secure Caesar's glorious mantle" (214). Cleopatra was well aware of Antony's goals, and she also knew that becoming Antony's ally would protect Egypt, since Antony was known for the strength of his army. The alliance was beneficial to both sides, and their futures became even more closely linked when the two became romantically involved. It was interesting to read about how both Cleopatra and Antony understood the practical side of their relationship, since most other historians place much more emphasis on their passionate love affair. Schiff instead describes this as a twelve-year burn, but does not dwell on their emotions, likely because there is great uncertainty in such speculation. The book provided insight into the way these figures actually lived instead of perpetuating the popular mythology of Antony and Cleopatra.

GRADE THE BOOK:

5 stars out of 5 – I loved reading this book. It was both well-written and contained much vigorously researched information. Whenever uncertainty did come up, Schiff did an excellent job analyzing the probabilities of possible explanations for gaps in the historical record. In the end, I came away feeling like I had gotten to know Cleopatra as a person. Rather than the stereotypical image of a manipulative seductress, I now see Cleopatra as an intelligent, gifted strategist, and one of the most influential women of the ancient world. In a universe where males ruled the political sphere, Cleopatra held her ground and led her own civilization to greater prosperity. Although some aspects of Cleopatra's story will remain shrouded in mystery, I feel that Schiff's book is the most comprehensive and informed biography possible.

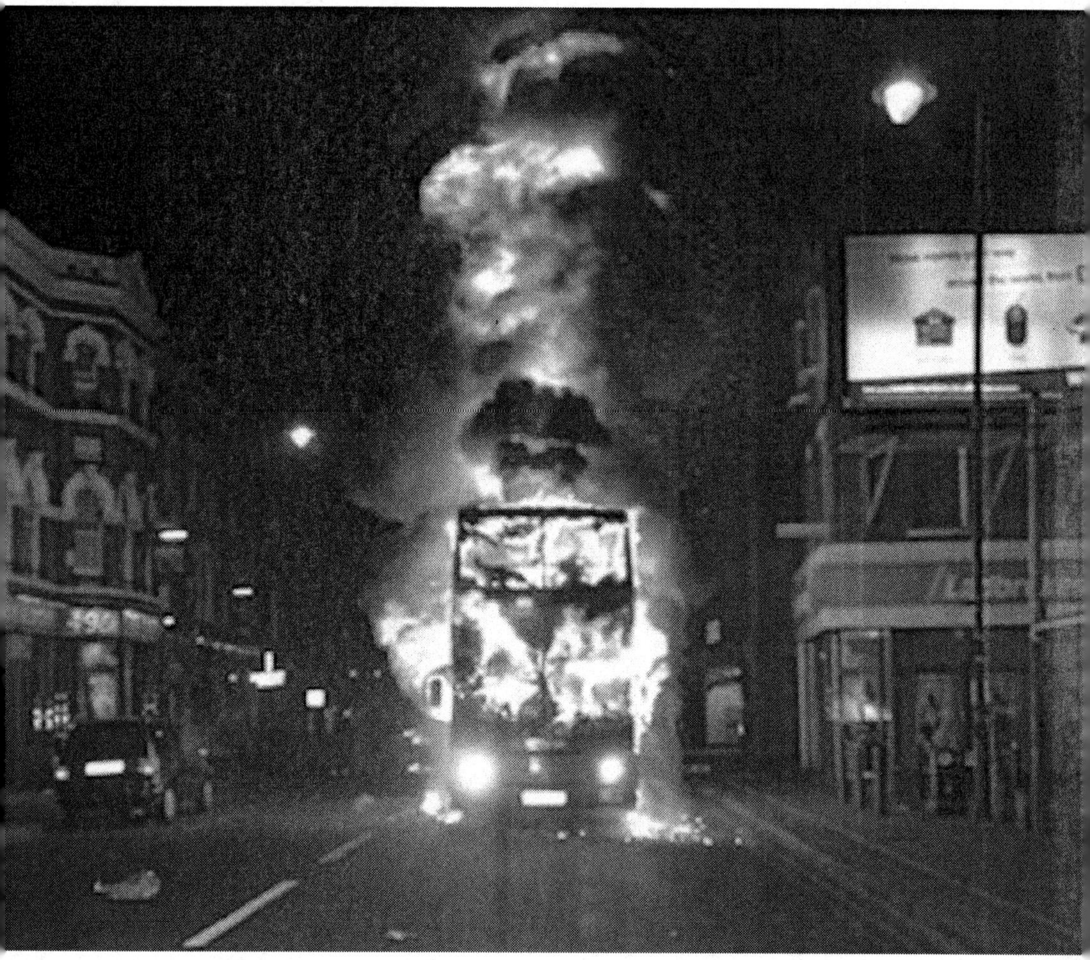

England Faces Aftermath of Violent Riots

Published by The Pulitzer Center

August 2011 became a chaotic month for England when an onslaught of riots battered the country. The first wave of violence struck in the aftermath of a peaceful protest march on August 6, during which a group of roughly 120 people walked across the North London district of Tottenham to show support for the family of Mark Duggan, a Tottenham resident who was shot by policemen on August 4. The police reportedly suspected Duggan of gang involvement, and claimed to have fired on Duggan because he himself was armed; they offered a police radio with a bullet wedged inside it as evidence.

Duggan's friends and family, however, insist that he was not armed after all, and so they chose to peacefully march on the Tottenham police station. Unsatisfied with the police response upon arrival at the station, the group of protesters became more vehement over time. Eventually, violence broke out when rumors spread that a policeman had attacked a sixteen-year-old girl.

By the end of the night, rioters had devastated Tottenham, vandalized and looted shops and even burned down public buildings, including the post office. Over the course of the next week, similar events of violence and vandalism raged throughout the entire United Kingdom, causing severe damage to major cities such as Birmingham and Edinburgh.

Who exactly were the rioters? The public belief appears to be that the majority of the rioters were teenage boys from poorer areas of England, but in reality, the looters greatly varied in age, ethnic background, and gender. The disparate group of rioters was unified by means of social media as television news ran constant coverage of where and when the violence was taking place. Facebook events spread the word about riot logistics, and text messages kept people up-to-date about the latest outbreaks. The majority of the riot hotspots, however, were in less affluent areas of the country, including cities like Manchester and Liverpool. In line with this trend, Tottenham has the highest unemployment rate of any London district and the eighth highest unemployment rate in the entire United Kingdom. This geographic distribution has fueled much discussion about the role of social class in the violence.

The harsher critics of the looters label their actions as opportunistic, fueled mainly by the desire to act out in a rare anarchic break from societal order. As the days passed, the riots may have become violent for the sake of violence. The rioters' plans spiraled out of control – at one point there was a plan in place to attack a children's hospital in Birmingham – and many English people find their actions to be unacceptable under any circumstances. Others view the rioters' actions from a more personal perspective. While riding in a London taxi a few days after the worst of the violence, I found myself in the midst of an involved discussion with the cabbie about the recent outbreaks. He explained to me that the class system in England has such clearly defined divisions between the affluent and the less fortunate that it is extremely difficult for people to climb the social ladder. While he was growing up, he experienced the hardships of growing up working class, one of which was the fact that he had to drop out of school to work and support his family. "On top of all that, I was born with the wrong [ethnic] last name, which made matters even more difficult," he said, referencing racism that he found inherent to daily life.

Although the cab driver found the scale of the violence to be both disturbing and deplorable, he insisted that most people did not understand how to view life in the United Kingdom from the perspective of the working class. There is an element of feeling trapped in a specific economic and social lifestyle, and there are not many opportunities for the lower classes to have a voice in the workings of their society, politically or otherwise. Indeed, unemployment is now at an astonishing high in the United Kingdom, 7.8%, and rioting may have been one of the only ways to catch mass attention in such a damaged system. As one Tottenham rioter told an NBC reporter, "You wouldn't be talking to me now if we didn't riot, would you? Two months ago we marched to Scotland Yard, more than 2,000 of us, all blacks, and it was peaceful and calm and you know what? Not a word in the press. Last night a bit of rioting and looting… and look around you."

Parliament was met with public criticism in the aftermath of the riots, as all senior ministers were enjoying their summer vacations during the first weekend of violence. Prime Minister David Cameron did not even depart Ibiza for London until the early hours of August 9, roughly three full days after the initial Tottenham outbreaks. Cameron stated that he did not want to create a "culture of fear" in England, but that he would be increasing police presence and increasing awareness of gang-fighting tactics among the officers. Even while passing through areas of the city that the police would not normally focus on, such as Westminster and Mayfair, I noticed multiple police officers stationed on busy street corners. All the same, Deputy Prime Minister Nick Clegg has made it clear that the government will not be rethinking their recent police budget cuts, and as a result, the near future will see the elimination of about 17,000 police jobs. According to Simon Reed of the England and Wales Police Federation, "If this happened next year, we could not cope with fewer officers."

By this point, the violence has come to an apparent end, but the residents of the affected areas are still rebuilding from the rubble and pushing forward in the emotional aftermath. Parliament has recently begun to discuss the implications of the riots in terms of the United Kingdom's class system, but only time will tell where these discussions will lead.

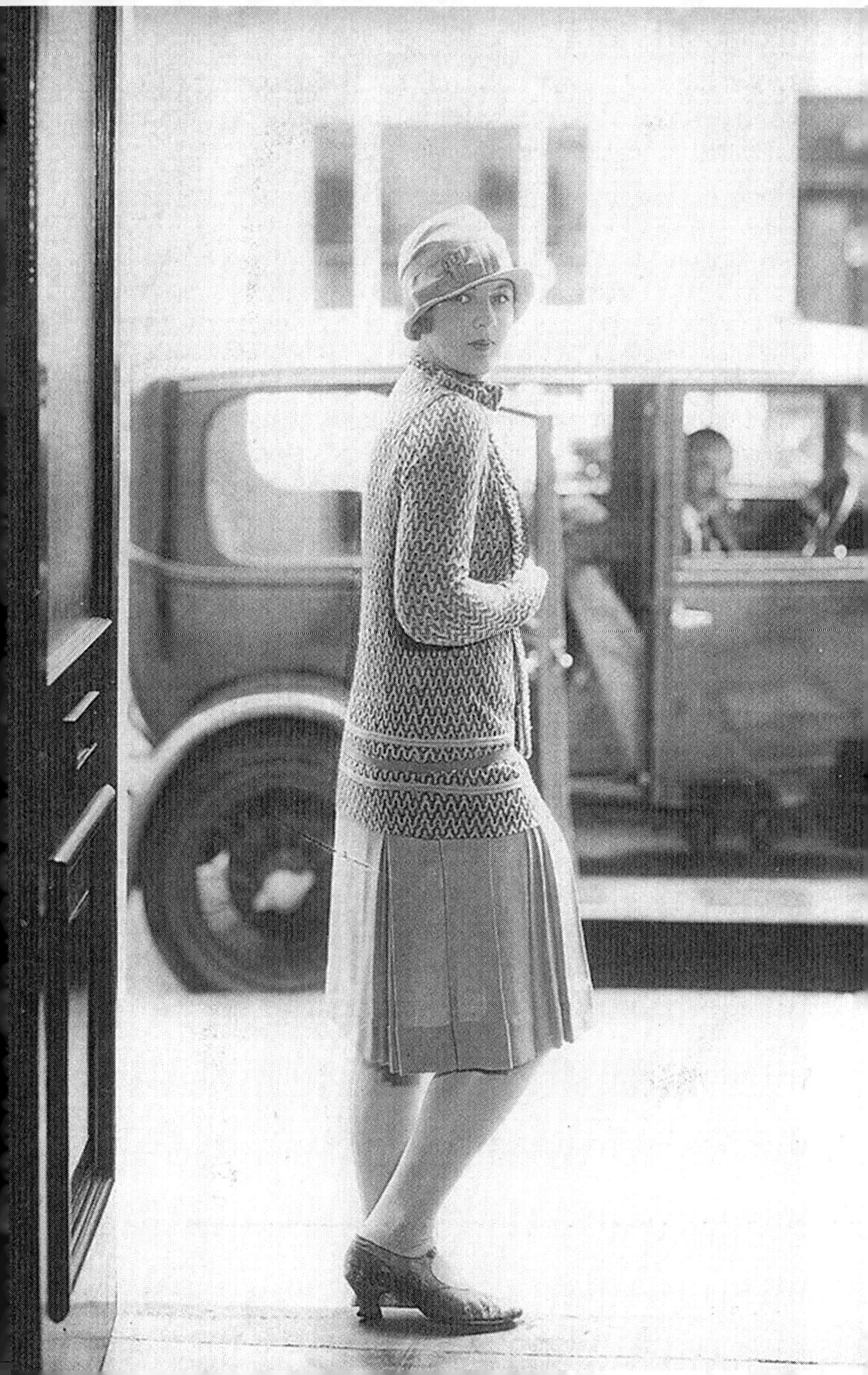

How the Youth Culture of the 1920s Reinvigorated America

Published by Op Ed News

Following the destruction caused by World War I, it became obvious that the United States needed to rebuild itself. Many long-held pre-war values and customs seemed irrelevant now, perhaps more so than ever before. Because of this, the youth of America began rebelling against many of the norms of their parents' generation as they strove to create something uniquely their own. Eventually, this new youth culture of the 1920s became the focus of a national obsession. Even adults played a part, with some attempting to imitate the new trends while others found themselves repulsed by them. But whatever adults of the time felt, they could not deny that the new world created by their country's youth was having a drastic effect on the American population as a whole. Though the defining characteristics of the movement may appear now to be fairly simple to pin down, the youth culture of the 1920s had synthesized new ideas of the post-war era with America's older traditions in such a way that a complex movement was created, reinvigorating the overall American population.

The ever-shifting trends of the new youth culture had defined it at its most basic level, but looking a bit deeper, it is clear that 1920s youth still wanted to retain some general values. The personas of the flapper and sheik for example personified the "flamboyant, reckless spirit" (Drowne and Huber 29) conjured up by common perceptions of this culture. Flappers and sheiks were the major trendsetters of the time, taking cues from films and other mediums of popular culture, believing their parents' generation to be "infinitely old-fashioned" (Drowne and Huber 30). They often would escape their houses in their cars to meet up with their peers, their equals. Though a cultural stereotype, such activity was often imitated not only by the youth but by adults as well who perceived the youth movement to be "fascinating" (Murray). What defined the youth culture in fact was constantly changing as trends shifted quite often. Popular culture was becoming a major force in American culture, and its youth now had new standards to keep up with in regards to popular music, fashion, dance crazes, and their appearance. Newspapers reported for example on which styles would take center stage in "the cycle of feminine fashions" ("Old-Time Shawls to Be Worn"). Keeping up to date with so many fads required both time and money for the youths. Though the flapper and sheik represented the cultural ideal, very few youths embodied all characteristics of such personas despite constantly striving to assume such roles.

Though the stereotype of this period seems fairly simple to understand, the reality of the culture itself is much more complex. While it wanted to take on the characteristics of the sheiks and flappers, America's youth also attempted to balance these new waves of trends with older pre-war values and traditions. Literary portrayals of women for instance often struggled to achieve such a balance. Though they found themselves "alienat[ed] from Victorian conceptions of home life" (Honey 27) and wanted to remain independent and break free from stereotypical, pre-war gender roles, this desire often took them "far away from the people-centered virtues of the family hearth" (Honey 32). Though the youth could date in their 20s, many still expected to settle down and marry when they grew older. Thus the definition of the youth culture exhibited much duplicity – the youth "appear[ing] to live on the cutting edge of social fashions while [they] privately maintain[ed] personal values that were far more traditional" (Drowne and Huber 47).

Even though the term "youth culture" suggests that the movement was purely youth-oriented, its influence percolated into older generations using college students as a starting point. The youth culture gained particular momentum through advertising, with those living in cities most greatly affected by its influence since they were the ones exposed to billboards and newspaper ads daily. Typically, trends from movies would be extended by college students who then spread them to high school students who "slavishly imitated" (Drowne and Huber 34) them. Those participating in college culture came to be regarded as the "chief arbiters of fashion and taste" (Drowne and Huber 35) a major component of what exactly the youth culture was. Additionally, adults would often attempt to imitate the new fads and "retain and preserve their youthful appearance" (Drowne and Huber 40), in a possible attempt to reconnect with elements of their past that they themselves missed. On the opposite side of the spectrum, other adults found themselves disgusted and repulsed by these new trends of the youth, "reproach[ing] them for their unconventional standards and inappropriate conduct" (Drowne and Huber 40). One New York Times journalist remarked frankly that "surely no one…would maintain that our 'flappers' are the worthy successors of the enchantresses of the past!" (Phillips). Both perspectives fueled the population's obsession with the youth movement, contributing to its overbearing influence on the social culture of the country.

Without new developments and inventions of the time, however, it is arguable that the youth movement could not have occurred in the first place. The automobile in particular revolutionized the way that American youth socialized, bestowing upon youth both "mobility and privacy" (Bailey 19) in a form that had never been available before. It became easier than ever for people to get around, abandoning their seemingly out-of-touch parents, as they sped around town to visit and socialize with their friends. Additionally, the car provided privacy in the sense that the youth were no longer under the constant watchful eye of their parents like youth had been during the age-old traditional system of dating referred to as "calling." As a result, dating became a more popular activity than ever before, the car helping with "accelerating and extending" (Bailey 19) this practice. The youth now had true independence thanks to the car, something teenagers constantly strove to attain as they matured but never attain the past so successfully.

Popular culture set the major standards for the youth to live up to, providing a method to advertise new trends and ideas. Movies, radio, advertising, and magazines popularized the idea of the flapper and the sheik, and also influenced the social conduct of the youth. From movies, people would learn what clothes were in fashion, a critical "benchmark by which American youth evaluated one another" (Drowne and Huber 43). Slang terms were also coined by movies – the movie The Sheik from 1921 introduced the defining word "sheik" to the population. In literature, feminism began to gain momentum as an actual movement. Motivated by the independent spirit of literary heroines, young women began to embrace this newfound sense of freedom and ambition. Though some disapproved, it became palpable that "the modern girl demands more freedom than her mother and grandmother did and, except in a few cases, she does not use that freedom unwisely" ("Modern Girl More Spirited"). The vast majority of the leading trends of the youth movement were established by popular culture.

The fads and interests of college students manifested the defining characteristics of the youth culture, propelling college students into the driver's seat of the movement. Sometimes the college culture would spread trends that they saw in movies and magazines, yet very often the way college students behaved would give popular culture itself new material. For example, many movies were based on university life, such as *The Freshman* and *Brown of Harvard*. As well, the magazine *College Humor* began to circulate, focusing "exclusively on the leisure activities of university students" (Drowne and Huber 34). People began to follow college sports teams, especially football, and students often went to watch football games every week or two as a result of the additional leisure time allowed by their schools. The social side of football games proved an immensely important component of the youth movement giving rise to the clichéd teenage obsession with popularity around this time. As college students began to use a rating-and-dating system, that is, a system of standards that evaluated people based on their social standings, it became clear that "success was popularity" (Bailey 27). Since college did not last forever, the youth could also take part in such superficial pastimes "without significant long-term risk" (Bailey 27). Despite this, the image of the college student became more and more significant in the formation of the American youth identity.

For a movement that held so much influence over the American population at the time, it is no surprise that many long-term effects were left behind in its wake, leaving drastic changes to American culture. It successfully reinvigorated for example not only the youth of the country, but the entire population, a necessary step to take following World War I's destruction because in this way, the youth movement created a method for cultural evolution – people now had the freedom to change the way life had previously been conducted in irrelevant war times. The youth now had more freedom and independence to socialize, allowing them to form a collective identity with their peers that captivated the nation. Additionally, gender roles were beginning to be re-defined, which paved the way for feminism to gain momentum. In this regard, it grew increasingly clear that many women possessed an "unwillingness to occupy the position assigned to [them]" (Honey 26). The idea that women were "seeking empowerment and declaring their right to express who they were as individuals" (Honey 39) was finally becoming more common. The 1920s youth movement thus presented the country with a quantity of new ideas that reshaped the standard American lifestyle.

Though this cultural reformation pushed America in the direction of the future, it also brought forth more complex issues for its participants to deal with. The country's "generation gap" widened as its youth "consciously… forg[ed] their own set of behavioral and moral codes" (Drowne and Huber 40) in order to separate themselves from their parents' generation. Yet these very same adults idolized them "in an effort to recapture the elusive qualities of youth" (Drowne and Huber 40), a phenomenon likely perpetuated by US advertising and media that "touted youthfulness as a commercial product that one could actually purchase" (Drowne and Huber 40). However, this purchasable youthfulness was the watered-down version of the youth movement, the stereotype of the flapper and the sheik that actually found close to no root in reality. Even though America's youth mainly strove for a clear break with the old-fashioned ideas of their parents' generations, they nonetheless attempted to retain traditional values in their lives. Women in particular found themselves faced with "two contradictory impulses…the desire to assimilate into the modern world and to flee from it, the rejection of a separate sphere for women and the fear of losing human connections" (Honey 26). Though they wanted to remain independent, many women still longed to settle down and start a family. Despite the fact that dating was becoming increasingly popular, "marriage allowed them to combine a sense of independence with a sense of security…in this system, though the competition might be fierce, one could win" (Bailey 47). Though far more traditional than anything the flapper represents, the marriage system made it impossible to pigeonhole the youth culture as purely breaking ties from the pre-war era, their struggle to balance tradition with their new lifestyle adding yet another layer to the movement's complexity.

The American youth movement of the 1920s set a new precedent for future generations. Members of the youth movement could embrace their independence and rebelliousness, but still eventually come to understand that they needed to hold on to at least some traditional values. The new shock waves of youthful fresh trends helped Americans push past the rubble left in World War I's shadow and look to the country's future. Though the youth movement may seem quite dated in the context of the modern world, today's world of 2010 may very well seem just as dated to future youth cultures, alienated as they may be from today's trendy habits and customs but still finding something in common with today's more sturdy traditions.

WORKS CITED

Bailey, Beth L. *From Front Porch to Back Seat: Courtship in Twentieth-Century America*. N.p.: John Hopkins University Press, 1989. Print.

Drowne, Kathleen, and Patrick Huber. *The 1920s*. Westport, Connecticut: Greenwood Press, 2004. Print.

Honey, Maureen. *Gotham's Daughters: Feminism in the 1920s*. N.p, n.p., n.d. Print.

"Modern Girl More Spirited, Service League Discovers." *The New York Times* 29 Mar. 1925: n. pag. Print.

Murray, Arthur. "Brains and the Flapper." Editorial. *The New York Times* 23 Dec. 1923: n. pag. Print.

"Old-Time Shawls to Be Worn, But With 'New Flapper Skirt.'" *The New York Times* 4 Feb. 1923: n. pag. Print.

Phillips, R. Le Clerc. "The Decline of Feminine Magic." *The New York Times* 7 Jan. 1923: n. pag. Print.

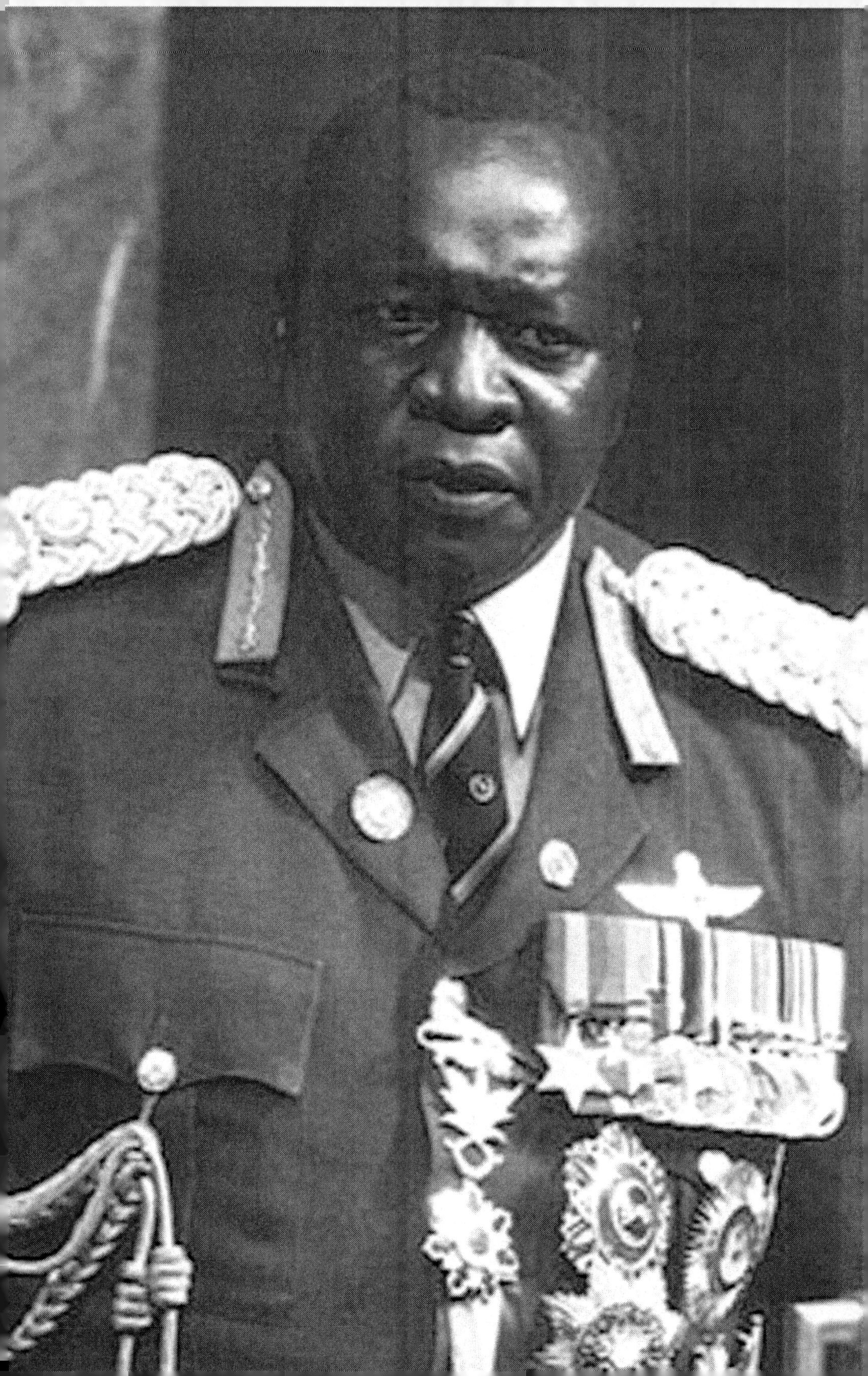

Idi Amin and the Tanzanian Invasion of Uganda: Research Memo

Research done for forthcoming book by Robert S. Litwak, Vice President for Programs and Director of International Security Studies at the Woodrow Wilson International Center for Scholars. Litwak is the author of the books Rogue States *and* Regime Change: U.S. Strategy Through the Prism of 9/11.

BACKGROUND:

Before he became such a heavily despised dictator, Idi Amin was in charge of both the Ugandan army and air force under Prime Minister Milton Obote. Between 1966 and 1971, Obote's relationship with Amin steadily crumbled to the point where Obote was preparing to arrest Amin for "misappropriating millions of dollars of military funds" (Harris). After becoming aware of Obote's plans, Amin decided to seize control of the Ugandan government in a violent military coup, all while Obote was out of the country for a Commonwealth Conference. This was met with positive reception from the Ugandans, as well as from the British and Israeli governments. However, perceptions of Amin and his plans for Uganda soon began to decay.

After Amin announced that he had received a message in a dream from God, he expelled all Israelis from Uganda as well as the majority of the Ugandan Asian population. Motivated to turn Uganda into "a black man's country," Amin stated that Britain should "take responsibility for all Asians in Uganda who are holding British passports, because they are sabotaging the economy of the country." In actuality, ordering the Asians to leave the

137

country meant destroying the backbone of Uganda's economy, since all of the Asian traders had been forced to leave. Not only did this action create a nightmare scenario for the Ugandan economy, it also lost Amin international support as it became increasingly obvious that Amin's regime was erratic and unpredictable.

THE INTERVENTION:

After Amin's coup, Obote fled to Tanzania. He was already good friends with Tanzanian leader Julius Nyerere, so Obote used Tanzania as a place to prepare his supporters to invade Uganda and oust Amin. He drew support from both the Tanzanians and the Sudanese. The Liberation War between Tanzania and Uganda came six years after an unsuccessful attempt to invade Uganda in 1972. The National Liberation Front, composed of Obote, his supporters, and Ugandan soldiers who had mutinied, was armed by the Chinese. In 1978, Amin learned that the National Liberation Front was planning to invade Uganda, so he prepared a counterattack and invaded Tanzania. The National Liberation Front was able to drive the invaders out of Tanzania and back into Uganda by December of 1978. In January, the National Liberation Front entered Uganda to remove Amin from power and restore peace to Uganda. Libya was the only country to attempt to intervene and aid Uganda. The Libyans were unable to fend off the Tanzanian troops - the morale of the Ugandan troops was steadily deteriorating. After the Tanzanians took control of Kampala in April of 1979, Amin resigned and fled to Libya.

THE AFTERMATH:

Though Nyerere himself ordered Tanzanian troops into Uganda to assist Obote with his efforts, he publicly insisted that his intentions were not to oust Amin himself - that was, in Nyerere's own words, "the right of the people of Uganda alone." Though Amin was chairman of the Organization of African Unity in 1975, he ended up embarrassing the organization more than helping it. He was only directly condemned by a few other African leaders, including Kenneth Kaunda of Zambia, who notably claimed that Amin was "as bad as Hitler."

Besides Libya, there was no external intervention with the invasion. The United Nations' opinion of Amin was clear after the murder of Ugandan Archbishop Janani Luwum and two ministers of the Ugandan cabinet in 1975 – President Jimmy Carter declared that the event had "disgusted the entire civilized world" and the British government even suggested that the U.N. intervene with Ugandan affairs. In 1977, African countries "blocked a United Nations resolution that would have condemned Amin for his gross violation of human rights" ("Idi Amin"). Idi Amin's regime left Uganda in shambles, a massive death toll and shocking national debt remaining in his wake.

REFERENCES:

Cooper, Tom, and Arthur Hubers. "Uganda and Tanzania, 1972-1979." *Central, Eastern, & Southern Africa Database.* N.p., 2 Sept. 2003. Web. 31 Dec. 2009. http://www.acig.org/artman/publish/article_187.shtml.

Harris, Bruce. "Idi Amin killer file." *More or Less: Heroes and Killers of the 20th Century.* N.p., 2 May 2007. Web. 31 Dec. 2009. http://www.moreorless.au.com/killers/amin.html.

"Idi Amin." *Encyclopedia of World Biography.* N.p., 2009. Web. 31 Dec. 2009. <http://www.notablebiographies.com/A-An/Amin-Idi.html>.

"Milton Obote - Times Online Obituary." *Times Online.* N.p., 12 Oct. 2005. Web. 31 Dec. 2009. http://www.timesonline.co.uk/tol/comment/obituaries/article1081268.ece.

"Uganda: Amin: The Wild Man of Africa." *Time Magazine Online.* N.p., 7 Mar. 1977. Web. 31 Dec. 2009. http://www.time.com/time/magazine/article/0,9171,918762-9,00.html.

"UGANDA: Big Daddy's Big Trouble." *Time Magazine Online.* N.p., 12 Mar. 1979. Web. 31 Dec. 2009. http://www.time.com/time/magazine/article/0,9171,948458-1,00.html.

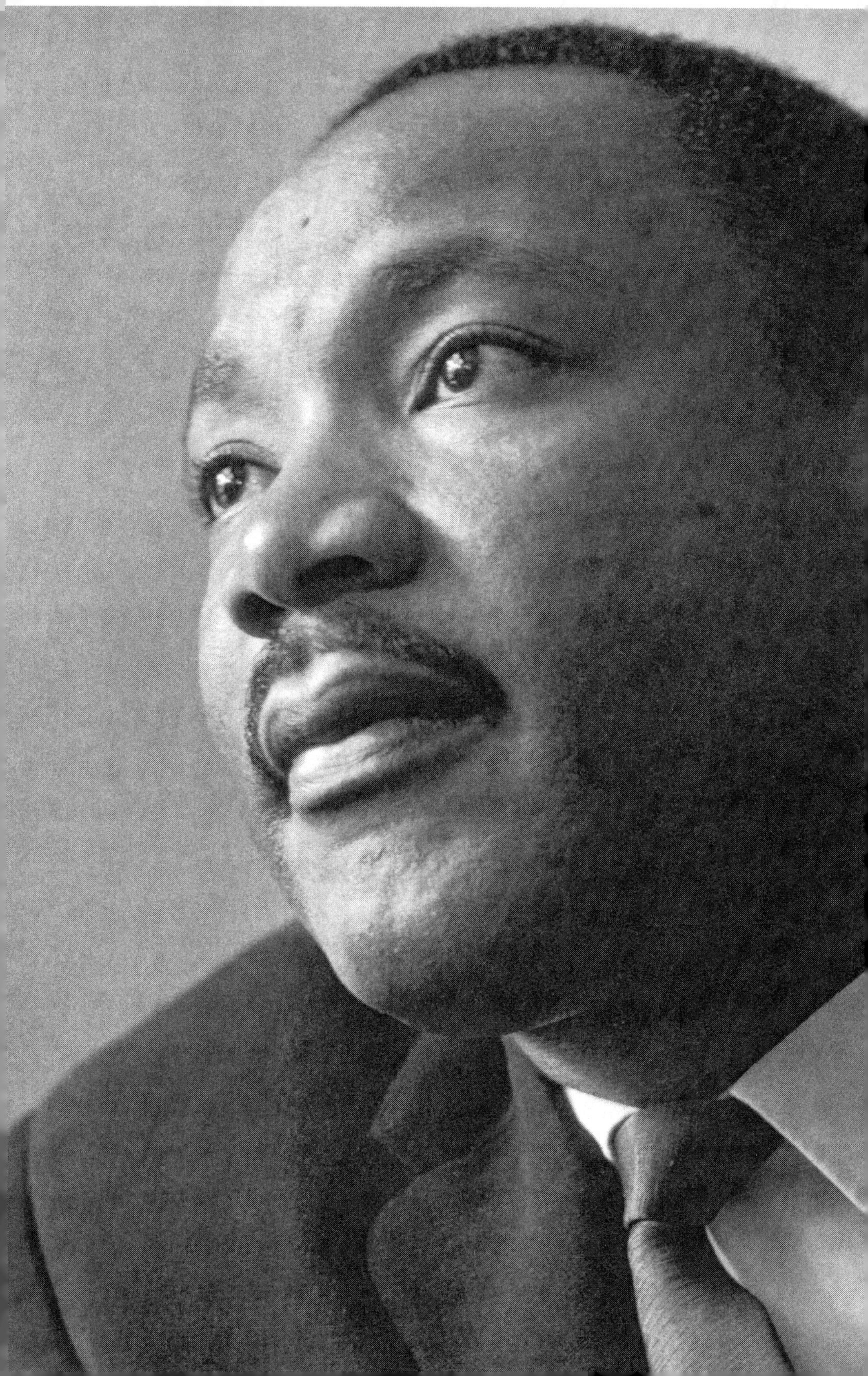

Letter from Birmingham Jail: Constructing the Optimal Argument

Published by Op Ed News

The ability to write a powerful persuasive piece results from total awareness of available rhetorical devices. Martin Luther King, Jr. demonstrates that he can effectively wield the sword of rhetoric in his famous *Letter from Birmingham Jail*. While imprisoned in Birmingham after leading a series of non-violent civil rights marches, King read a letter in the city's newspaper that the city clergymen had written to him. The piece was entitled "A Call for Unity," and it suggested that King cease his protesting and wait to peacefully negotiate rights for African-Americans. Immediately, King began to draft a response piece on the very newspaper he was reading, a piece that would outline for critics why his actions of civil disobedience were essential and why it was necessary that more people, particularly white moderates, should be motivated to actively campaign for African-American rights. This piece, *Letter from Birmingham Jail*, showcases King's attention to distance, sentence structure, and overall tone as he balances the three appeals to prove his point.

Varied sentence structures allow King to build his argument in ways that appeal to both logos and pathos. Particularly notable is his usage of sharp, succinct balanced sentences, which serve a dual purpose as extremely emphatic statements and extremely quotable statements. These balanced sentences often appear at the very end of a section of concrete explanation, serving as a short summary of King's point. Near the beginning of the essay,

King confirms that he is "cognizant of the interrelatedness of all communities and states," using this as a reason why he felt it necessary to travel to Birmingham for a protest. He ends this thought with a concise balanced sentence: "Injustice anywhere is a threat to justice everywhere." Because strong logical reasoning reinforces these sentences, they carry considerable force and help the reader fully absorb his point. This also contributes to King's ethos, making him seem very knowledgeable and therefore very credible and persuasive.

While King's logic is integral to the success of his piece, he does not lose sight of the value of pathos. One of the highlights of King's essay is a lengthy paragraph on the third page concerning the way African-Americans have waited for their rights. The majority of the paragraph is a drawn-out periodic sentence which lays out struggles that African-Americans face, including the image of a six-year-old girl with "ominous clouds of inferiority beginning to form in her little mental sky" because of segregation, and the sight of "twenty million Negro brothers smothering in an airtight cage of poverty in the midst of an affluent society." The tension of the sentence builds and builds until the final clincher statement – "then you will understand why we find it difficult to wait." The African-Americans waited and waited for the day when they would finally be granted Constitutional rights; yet, that day never came, thus locking them into an endless cycle of suffering. This periodic sentence translates a brief version of this cycle into writing. He forces readers themselves to wait uncomfortably for the sentence to draw to a close, but once it does, King's ending statement becomes all the more powerful. The sentence generates a visceral emotional response as an effective appeal to the audience's emotion.

The distance created by King's tone closes the gap between him and his audience, and in so doing adds to the persuasive nature of his piece. Since this piece is, first and foremost, a letter, King realizes that he must directly address his initial audience of a few Birmingham clergymen. He extends polite compliments to the clergymen, referring to them as "men of genuine good will" and acknowledging that their criticisms were likely "sincerely set forth." King chooses to use very polite, formal diction when addressing them, since he realizes that he must persuade the clergymen to think highly of him if he wants them to even attempt to understand his points. He engages directly with the clergymen, addressing specific pieces of their argument to show that he has taken their ideas into deep consideration. Yet, King understands that the piece must work both ways, and so he uses rhetorical questions to provoke the clergymen to consider his own ideas on the subject. When discussing the way to distinguish between just and unjust laws, King walks the clergymen through a variety of different concrete examples, quoting philosophers such as Buber and Tillich and explaining how "any law that degrades human personality is unjust." After laying out his evidence, King directly asks the reader, "is not segregation an existential expression of man's tragic separation, his awful estrangement, his terrible sinfulness?" This powerful inquiry forces his audience to confront their preconceived notions about just and unjust. King likely intended that this rhetorical question cause the clergymen to step away from their own ideas as they engaged with his own.

King's dramatic shift in tone near the end of the letter is the final indicator of his ability to completely understand his audience. While the first half of the essay features polite diction as King responds to the clergymen's claims, the second half of the letter becomes more accusatory as he begins to directly address what he believes to be his audience's shortcomings. In particular, King discusses his "grave disappointment" with white moderates, the ones who tell the African-Americans to merely wait for the government to grant them their rights. King retaliates that these people live "by a mythical concept of time" and have "shallow understanding" of the true issue at hand, cinching his argument with the claim, "lukewarm acceptance is much more bewildering than outright rejection." Though the clergymen are calling for negotiation, they are also implying that the African-Americans should passively wait to be granted their rights, which places them in the white moderate category that King so vehemently critiques. Since King initially uses polite diction to persuade the clergymen to carefully examine his point of view, he realizes he now has some freedom to begin edging towards definite critiques of their actions. King goes on to voice his disappointment with the church itself, calling it an "arch defender of the status quo" - a body who protects the stagnant nature of ideas for society, a body that is standing in the way of the change he is fighting for. As a reverend himself, King makes it clear that this disappointment could not exist "where there is not deep love," and that he still "sees the church as the body of Christ." This type of religious language shows that King is aware of his audience's religious leanings, and thus realizes he must not completely alienate them if he wants his points to get across. King ends his discussion of the church by stating that he hopes "the church as a whole will meet the challenge of this decisive hour," calling his fellow clergymen to rise to the occasion and assist his efforts in the Civil Rights Movement. King's awareness of his audience dictates the way that he paces his writing, therefore allowing him to lay out an argument specifically designed for their benefit.

King's control of rhetorical strategies helps him to construct the optimal argument for his point of view. He pays attention to critical details and keeps in mind the leanings of his audience. At the same time, King also keeps in mind that this piece can appeal to a broader audience than just the clergymen, giving him an opportunity to voice his opinions on one of the most substantial issues of the day. His call to action simply *needed* to be articulated as strongly as possible in order to increase momentum. King's talent as a writer and orator granted him the ability to be so influential during this critical moment in history. *Letter from Birmingham Jail* is thus an accurate and representative reflection of his strength.

MISCELLANEOUS

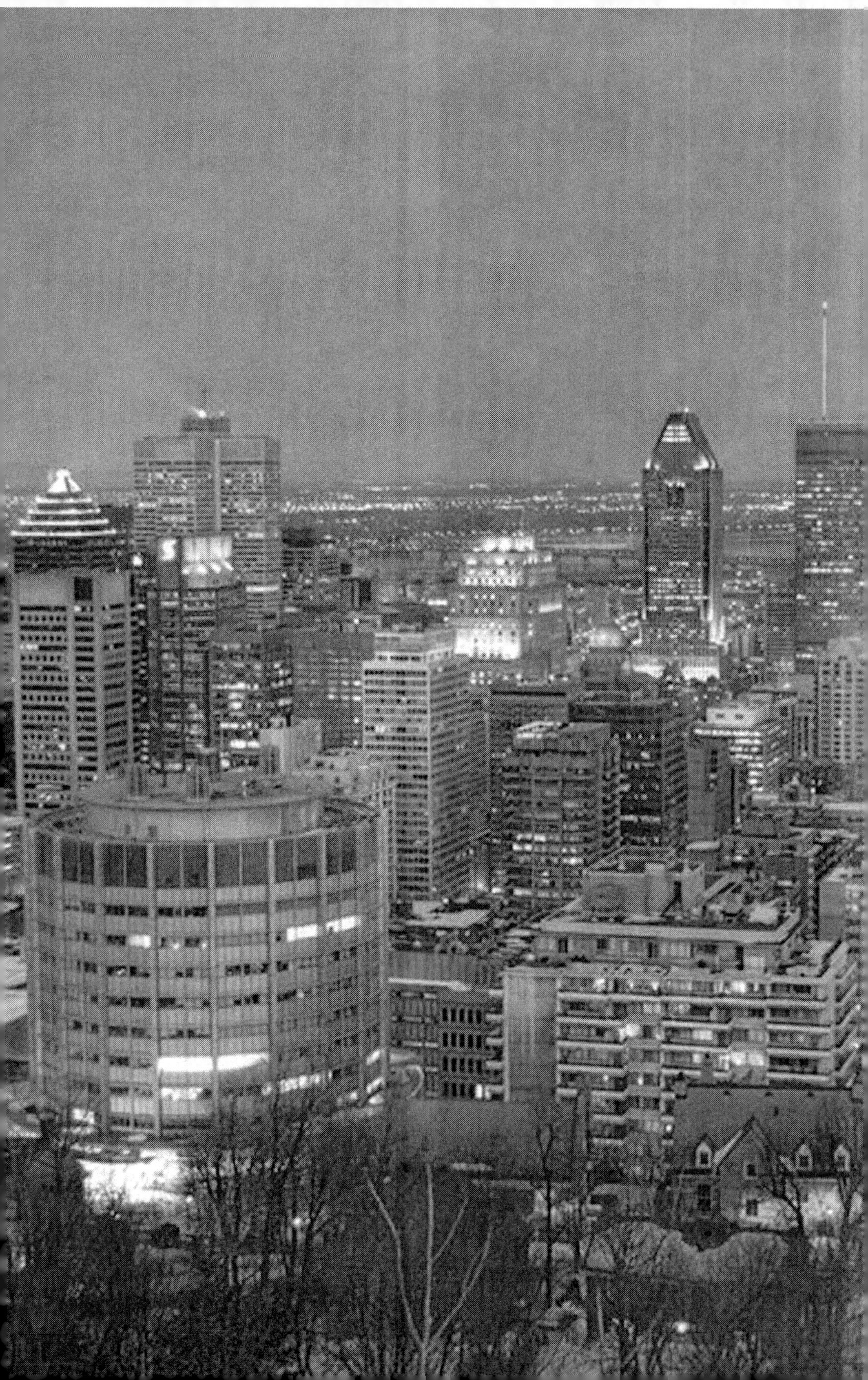

A Tale of Montreal: Reflections on a Seventh Grade Class Trip

Published in The Concord Journal *as the winning submission for a French class essay competition*

I can still remember the day when I learned that our French class would be the first seventh grade class to be able to travel to Montreal for three days. I was starry-eyed and excited as high expectations whirled around in my head. And now, after the trip is over, it all feels like a dream. The trip raised the bar miles above where I had set it. Thousands of memories have made a home in my mind, there to stay for the rest of my life.

There was never a dull moment while we were in Montreal. There was always something for us to do, whether it was going to places like Notre-Dame Basilica and the Underground City or having a tour of the city on the "moach," which was our name for the motor coach bus we rode around in during our stay. The one activity that stood out the most for me was the "18th century adventure" we embarked on the first night we were there. We visited an actual 18th century fort where we were transported back to the 1700s for a couple hours. We had to solve the mystery of the mysterious man in black who was running around in the shadows while trudging through a dark forest in the freezing Canada cold. We were all transformed into French soldiers in training who were posing as Swedish slaves immediately upon arrival at the fort. When the climatic shots at the end of it all were ringing out, I was filled with the type of fear you get when you go into a haunted house at a theme park – you're afraid, but the adrenaline rushing through your body makes the experience exciting and all the more fun. The actors did a great job of making you feel like you're actually living in the time period that the adventure takes place in, and I could see history come alive more than the textbooks in school ever did for me. Trekking through the woods on that cold night is something I'll remember for a long time.

When we arrived in Montreal on the moach, the difference that was most apparent to me was how much French I saw in the city. All of the signs were written in French and everyone I ran into spoke fluent French – I couldn't hear any English being used on the sidewalks apart from the other kids from Concord, leading their own conversations a few feet away from me. At first, I thought the language barrier would be the hardest part about the trip, but I found myself relying on the French I learned in school and was able to pick up a few more words. I don't think I would have learned as much if the people didn't speak quite as much French – the amount they spoke was the perfect amount for me to learn from. Montreal is one of the best places to go if you want to expand your French vocabulary.

And now for the part of my somewhat lengthy article that most other students dread having to write – the part about how my "window onto the world" is changing. Whenever it's announced that we have to write about this in class, everyone groans. So I'm going to be brave and talk about my "window" without complaining. In Montreal, I was exposed to a new culture. I learned from the experience that not every country speaks in the same tongue, but you don't have to whine about not knowing what the people are saying. You can try and learn some new words or phrases to use while you're there. That knowledge makes the difference and immerses you even more in the culture. The little cultural differences between nations are what make our world so special – different areas on the same blue and green sphere can be polar opposites, and I'm not just talking about the north and south poles. The different languages, cuisines, and fashions all over the planet define who we are. I had heard people say this before I went to Montreal, but I never really experienced it. And now I can say firsthand that my window onto the world has broadened its view on cultural differences and I've realized how vital they are to making our world interesting.

At the top of the world's tallest inclined tower, rising 574 feet above its home city, Montreal, I looked down to see the small buildings below, their dwarfish heights trumped by the mammoth structure I was standing in. I had to be on top of the world. I peered out at the breathtaking skyline, and I realized that I didn't see buildings that were new to my eyes. I saw all the memories of the trip that had occurred throughout the city, the memories that I would hold with me for years and years afterward, warm and familiar. I knew that the Montreal trip was the best school trip I had ever been on and it was utterly unforgettable. I thought to myself, *Nothing is going to beat this*. And now I'm positive that I was right.

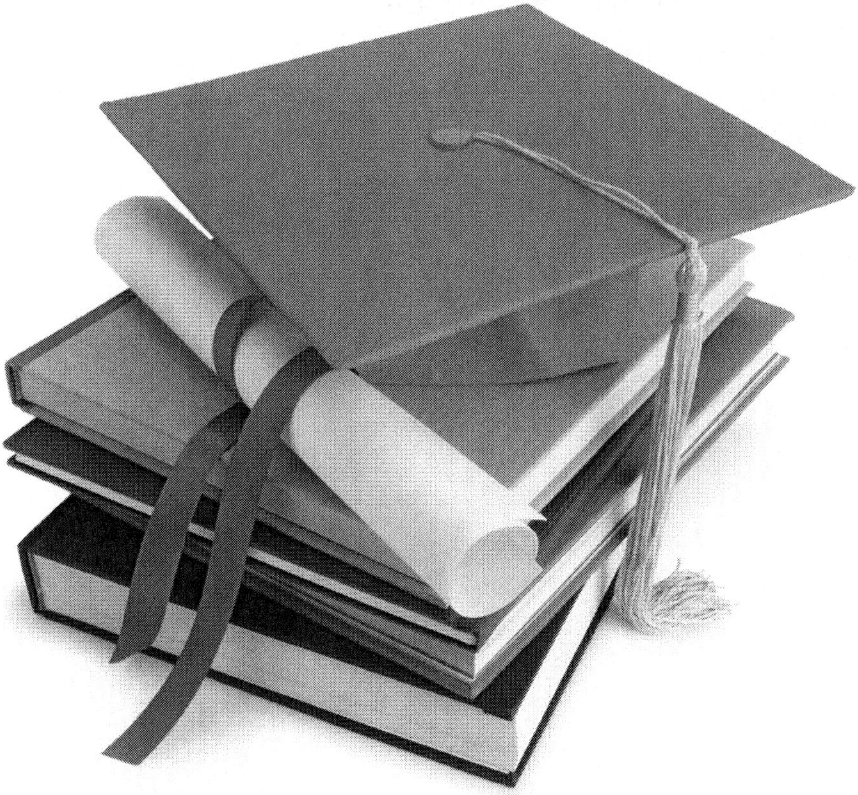

Competing with the System Itself: A Speech

Published by Op Ed News

AN ADDRESS TO THE LOCAL SCHOOL BOARD:

Good afternoon, everyone. I know you might have come here today expecting me to rattle off a never-ending list of critiques at you. You might be anticipating an awkward few minutes complete with uncomfortable fidgeting, and maybe even secondhand embarrassment for me. Let me assure you right away that my argument is not about all of you – this is about the system. The system is the one to blame, and also the one we should work together to fix. This is something that the student body and I cannot accomplish without your help, so I'd appreciate your attention as I explain the issues at hand.

Let me put you in the right frame of mind before I begin. For a few minutes, pretend you're no longer an adult. Pretend you're a contemporary high school student. Pretend you're still passing through those crucial years of self-consciousness and self-involvement, and pretend that you are facing the endless cycle of high school life. Maybe you run track, maybe you DJ a radio show, maybe you're the captain of the varsity curling team. No matter who you are, you still face the same cycle of monotony that is high school's trademark. From roughly 6 AM until 11 PM, you face every single stress factor imaginable. It's your job to balance a social life with your extracurriculars, and don't ever forget to spend countless hours working on homework. That seven-letter word spelled c-o-l-l-e-g-e becomes the one word you never want anyone to say ever again. And, sadly, you find yourself excited if you get seven hours of sleep. This is daily life.

Now, it might be easy to dismiss this cycle by labeling it "life." And, yes, these are stereotypical examples. It's unrealistic to believe that we can live without ever facing any stress. However, I definitely believe that it is possible for us to improve the system. Let the high school students battle only four million different types of stress, instead of four million and one.

In high school, there is an emphasis on competition that I believe is toxic. I don't mean competition with other students over grades, I mean competition with the system itself. The student is forced into difficult classes in the name of "impressing" admissions officers, slaving through hours and hours of extra work that is not necessarily enjoyable. You rarely encounter a seventeen-year-old who would say, "I'm so pumped to work on my trigonometry homework!" Besides, that one rare student was probably accepted to M.I.T. at age thirteen. This demand for "challenging," "impressive" classes make high school seem like an irrepressible vise. To what extent do the students' interests come through in their schedule? And who can actually judge what subjects are most valuable to the learning process? I understand the need for a well-rounded education, but there comes a point where students should be able to craft their education to suit their own interests. Phrases like "impressive to admissions officers" should be the last thing on students' minds.

And what are all these "impressive" classes worth if they lack personal meaning? What is anything worth without personal meaning? I can be applauded for learning the correct way to find the limit of a quadratic function, but it doesn't mean that I've learned anything I would personally think is useful. I'm not about to run home and start graphing for fun, and I definitely don't see this knowledge becoming useful later on in my life. If any of you on the board are into math, I'd like to apologize right now – it's probably quite apparent I am not one of you. If you want to run home and prove some trig identities, that's great, but maybe you hate interpreting poetry, or learning to master an instrument. If you were in high school right now, you wouldn't understand why those subjects mattered because they simply would not be meaningful to you.

This, o school committee, is one thing the public education system desperately needs. The freedom for students to choose. Instead of feeling boxed into rigid academic paths, students should have free space on their schedule to devote to exploring their own interests. A larger independent project program could solve this problem. An opportunity for students to do something entrepreneurial and personally significant would offset the meaningless demands of other academic subjects. This would need to extend beyond senior project and be offered to underclassmen. An open-ended project would foster individuality, creativity, and enthusiasm. Students should not be concerned about what school demands from them, they should be concerned about what they can demand from their school.

I know what some of you may be thinking right now. I have just suggested that you add an entire project to the normal course load of high school students. Doesn't this create even more stress? The answer is: Yes. With the current system in place, of course this would add more weight to the normal five tons of nightly paperwork. Yet, there is still a necessity for us to have a project we can look forward to working on. A project under our own control. A project that is not a key element of the cycle of burnout.

The cycle of burnout is at the root of the high school student's struggle. Constant work. Constant lack of sleep. Constant lack of control. In most of my required classes, the demands seem to be much more important than the content. Honors students are simply rewarded for their efforts through more work to complete. Our normal course loads demand so much time from us that I often wonder if the faculty understands that we have, you know, lives to live. We have other things going on in our lives besides school. It's not an excuse of a slacker, it's just a fact. School is a constant struggle between the desire to succeed and the continual stress. An existential crisis is a common symptom – after three hundred papers and four thousand problem sets, what does this all mean? We are not in school to learn, we are in school to be evaluated.

As I've said, this is our life. This is the reality. But, with your cooperation and input, we can change this. We can lessen some of the stress. Understanding our flawed system is the first step towards changing it. Like anything else, the system will never be perfect, but it can definitely be improved. We want to accomplish this through collaboration. Only you can help us make official changes to the way things are. And, because of this, there will need to be some give and take. We are mature enough to deserve some respect, and calling our concerns "trivial" would be nothing short of insulting. The attempted repression of the CCHS Sleep-In, for example, was insulting. You must understand our complaints are valid, and in return, we will accept that wild system overhauls are not entirely realistic. But let us begin to improve the system together.

THIS IS PROBABLY THE FIRST TIME ANYONE EVER RESTED BY TAKING A BEATING-- BUT THEN, I NEVER WAS MUCH OF A CONFORMIST!
CAN'T WAIT MUCH LONGER --I'M BEGIN-NING TO ACHE!
9

Unique at All Costs: An Editorial on the Individual

Published by Teen Ink

Non-conformism is a way of life. It encapsulates much more than just the idea of refusing to conform. In fact, refusing to conform is a deceptively challenging task. How is it possible to avoid society's influence to the degree that one may emerge unaffected by any mainstream trends? Tough task, but non-conformism is a mold that you can fit into with a bit of effort. Since the term itself is bland and vague, analyzing the actual tactics of non-conformists may help to define the philosophy more clearly.

Non-conformism means staying ahead of the trend. It is that moment after someone casually remarks that they enjoyed watching a popular new movie the past weekend, and you are able to look them dead in the eye and say, "I have been waiting to see that movie since I first heard about it two years ago…before anyone else knew about it." Written on the page, this final remark seems unnecessary. The Times New Roman drips with passive aggression. Yet some version of that detail is usually never left unsaid. Those final six words automatically grant one the cultural edge. Before the hype, before the masses of people flocked to the theater to watch that movie, cultural eons before any of this began, you heard about this film and concluded that it would be an interesting movie to see. You were never swept away by any mainstream trend. In fact, one could argue that you created the trend. This knowledge automatically bestows satisfaction and superiority. Never mind that no pedestals actually exist for hipsters to stand on – as a non-conformist, you have earned the right to tell everyone in your life that you were the first one to know.

Non-conformists must remain unique at all costs. Starting trends is one way to do so, but avoiding popular trends is another essential activity. That band may have been your favorite when only ten other people in the United States knew its first album, but what happens when that band writes a hit single and everyone within a mile of your house is able to sing along with the chorus? What if awareness of that band is no longer a marker of one's impeccable taste in obscure music? There is only one logical answer to this question. Your professional relationship with those musicians has officially come to an end. In order to be an individual, it does not make sense to continue listening to something so mainstream. Toss those beloved demo recordings and B-sides out the window. There has to be an underground act that is just as good, or at least halfway there. Quality is irrelevant when indie credibility is at stake. There is, of course, a gray area when it is just as much a trend to dislike something as it is to like it. What to do when it seems impossible to avoid conforming? Think for a moment. "…I've never heard of Justin Bieber." Perfect response.

Non-conformism relies on the importance of the individual. Avoiding trends so diligently may make it difficult to find any common interests you share with people whom you encounter on a day-to-day basis. For this reason, the non-conformist tends to lead a solitary life. They are the ones sporting "Je suis Morrissey" t-shirts and carrying well-worn copies of *The Catcher in the Rye*. However, this does not bother them, since they quite enjoy this independence. In fact, it provides them with a sense of accomplishment. As a non-conformist, you should take pride in your strength of self, as you rely purely on your own instincts to construct your own identity. Ordering edgy, mass-produced clothes should make a statement that you stand alone in your fashion sense. Scouring Pitchfork's website to read the reviewers' opinions of the latest trends in alternative music should contribute to your vibrant, impressive CD collection. Neglecting any outside influence is intrinsic to the non-conformist. You should scoff at others' attempts to categorize you, to label you. You are, after all, An Individual.

Non-conformism ultimately entails indifference towards others' opinions of your identity. The way others perceive you is meaningless. Your interests and viewpoints should convey the crux of your distinctive personality, the defining factor that sets you apart from the rest. All of your efforts in crafting your persona should serve to further distinguish yourself. At the same time, it is important that everyone around you is very much aware of how special you are. So, plaster those clever philosophical aphorisms all over the info section of your Facebook. Showcase your creativity. Yes, of course you can recycle an old John Lennon quote…just change a few words, rearrange the sentence structure, and it is automatically your own.

"This is a delicious evening, when the whole body is one sense, and imbibes delight through every pore. I go and come with a strange liberty in Nature, a part of herself."

—"Solitude," page 1

Thoreau Challenge: Journal Entries Inspired by Henry David Thoreau's *Walden*

Published by Teen Ink

I have only attempted this once before in my life, roughly ten years ago. An eight-year-old Chloe sprung up the unforgiving gradient, breath condensing in the mid-December frost. I caught my breath at the top while gazing out across the Massachusetts vista, Walden Pond frozen over as a rare break in the sea of trees.

Now I am seventeen, and I find that my muscles are not exactly conditioned to running up a nearly vertical slope. I slog through the muggy air usually associated with a July afternoon rather than the beginning of October. After what seems like an eon, I reach the top, a grassy plateau dotted by blue candy cane drainage pipes. I collapse next to one of them, all muscles slackening as the deep cloudless blue monopolizes my sense of sight. My dry throat craves a water bottle from the ice cream truck in the Walden Pond parking lot. My worst-case scenario survival instinct kicks into gear. *What if I passed out from dehydration up here? Would anyone find me until next week?*

I am struck by the isolation of such a place. Before long, Pine Hill's summit feels like my own grassy expanse. Only I am witness to the sights and sounds of this space during this brief period of time. It is a type of ownership that cannot be expressed to others. As I start to recuperate, I am lulled into serenity. I could have spent ten minutes there or two hours – time seems irrelevant.

Calmness in nature may appear to imply silence, but Pine Hill is not a natural vacuum. I overhear the incessant chirping of insects, the chattering of birds, even the noise of motors on the road below. A hawk glides through my field of vision, and an airplane crosses over while descending into Hanscom. There is activity.

Peace in nature is not found in complete stillness or silence, but it is found in feeling attuned to an ancient dimension that shifts as dynamically as society. The forces inherent to nature overcome me without much effort on my part – I only needed to relax and listen. There is something rejuvenating in allowing a world so simple to flow through your veins. All of my modern stresses and problems are distant from my mind, and wordless thought fills the voids. Like Thoreau, I am "distinctly made aware of the presence of something kindred" in the "infinite and unaccountable friendliness" ("Solitude" 3) of this world.

Revived, I stand up and search for a gap in the trees to look out across the state landscape. The trees have not shed their foliage yet, so I can only glimpse half of Walden Pond. The outline of Wachusett Mountain stands ghost-like in the distance. It is not what I remember, but I am not disappointed. I have already been rewarded for my struggle to reach the top. My vivid memory of the view from Pine Hill's summit first drew me to explore this place again, but there are unobservable secrets here that will encourage me to return.

> *"Both place and time were changed, and I dwelt nearer to those parts of the universe and to those eras in history which had most attracted me. Where I lived was as far off as many a region viewed nightly by astronomers."*
>
> — "Where I Lived and What I Lived For," page 5

II – WALDEN

I decide to go for a walk around Walden Pond itself to reacquaint myself with where Thoreau lived. I cannot even remember the last time I took the forty-minute walk around the pond, despite the fact that I am a Concord resident. There are many others who have decided that today would be the ideal day to visit the pond, as well. The beach area is overrun with families who have decided to go for a swim in the famous pond, and there are a few lonely fishermen patiently waiting on the shore for a fish to snatch their lines. I pass by this activity as I begin my circuit.

The path traces the edge of the pond, and I can't help continually observing the water from different angles. The soft current bobs up and down with comforting regularity. Trees tower from all sides, their foliage beginning to assume vibrant orange hues as winter approaches. I can imagine the forest continuing uninterrupted for countless miles across the state, when suddenly this tranquil splash of blue disturbs the network of trees. It is an enclosure from the world, an oasis. Although I rationally know that Concord center is only a mile away, Walden feels psychologically light years away from civilization.

Eventually, I arrive at Thoreau's cabin site, spotting the pile of rocks memorializing his endeavor to "live deliberately" ("Where I Lived…" 7). Once more, I am not alone - tourists snap pictures of their children on top of the rock pile. I walk over to the stones marking the foundation of Thoreau's cabin site, looking out at the pond. I envision Thoreau's view from his cabin window at dawn, the sun glimmering off the snippet of water visible between the trees. Natural beauty at Walden is palpable. I can easily understand how Thoreau could lose himself in this environment. The minutiae of human existence are meaningless when faced with such indescribable yet obvious splendor. What is life worth if people never take the time to go outside and connect with something so seemingly obvious? I remember Thoreau's comment that the poet enjoys "the most valuable part of a farm" ("Where I Lived…" 2), while the farmer lives concerned with his work. I am not sure Thoreau would argue that the farmer is not doing work that is necessary to society's existence, but I can now understand what he was attempting to convey. Nature's magic seems so painstakingly obvious when visiting a place like Walden, and it is frustrating to think of how many people miss out on this aspect of life. To appreciate nature is to momentarily forget the concerns of life, and Thoreau's farmer does not take the time to do so.

My walk around Walden is an escape. I am experiencing, rather than feeling compelled to translate my observations into words. Perhaps words are not essential to discovering the necessities of life. I felt all I needed to know.

> "I find it wholesome to be alone the greater part of the time. To be in company, even with the best, is soon wearisome and dissipating. I love to be alone. I never found the companion that was so companionable as solitude. We are for the most part more lonely when we go abroad among men than when we stay in our chambers."
>
> — "Solitude," page 4

III – EMERSON'S CLIFF

I return to Walden with the desire to explore beyond the beaten path. Before my attempt, I wander over to the replica of Thoreau's cabin in the parking lot. I should sign the guestbook. My plans are curtailed by the amount of tourists flitting in and out of the cabin. Children climb on the Thoreau statue guarding the cabin's entrance. People take pictures of themselves sitting on the cabin's twin bed to post on Facebook later that evening. People even discuss whether or not Walden was a work of fiction, and that Thoreau simply invented his cabin escapades to validate his philosophical musings. I find myself simultaneously uncomfortable and confused, so I decide to cross the street to the pond before I can even enter the cabin.

The idea of tourists visiting my hometown has always fascinated me. I am aware on some level that Concord is a landmark in both American and literary history, but I am always surprised to see amorphous tour groups snapping pictures throughout town. Too often, I forget how easily I can overlook this aspect of home, and I wish I had a more conscious appreciation for it.

About a third of the way around the pond, I spot a trail extending up a hill into the woods. Perfect. I follow it away from the central pond. After about half a mile of trekking alone through non-descript woodland, I arrive at the entrance to a path forking off to the left. A sign informs me that this is the entrance to "Emerson's Cliff."

As I begin to walk this path, I remember my father telling me that Emerson used to write in seclusion at a specific place in Walden Woods named Emerson's Cliff. I imagine Emerson walking up this very same hill in his stiff, formal suit, clutching a stack of papers as he navigated the rocky incline. It is difficult to picture figures like Emerson in the great outdoors, as central as nature is to transcendentalist writings.

In hindsight, Emerson's Cliff should have been named Emerson's Hill, but I can understand that a hill does not quite capture the same essence of drama as a cliff. The trees obscure any view of Walden Pond, and seemingly generic woodland extends into the distance on all sides. There is a lone boulder resting on its peak, which makes a perfect seat. Without a doubt, Emerson sat on this very boulder to compose his essays, and I soon understand why. I feel like I have melded into the landscape like I did at Pine Hill, and I function as a component of nature rather than a mere observer. The same sense of peace overwhelms me, in contrast to the unease I experienced among the masses at the cabin replica. There is clarity of thought associated with solitary immersion in nature, and I am sure that Emerson sought this lucidity when he came to write at this very location. In this brief separation from societal influence, Emerson would have been able to look inward and give verbal form to his philosophy in "Self-Reliance." As Thoreau claimed, nature communicates true reality, and "if we respected only what is inevitable and has a right to be, music and poetry would resound along the streets" ("Where I Lived…" 9).

This is my third nature experience, and I wonder why I have not had many unique, consciously philosophical thoughts of my own. In order to think as deeply as Thoreau or Emerson did, it is necessary to completely immerse oneself in nature, and one-hour fragments of time here and there are simply not enough to have these sorts of insights. I need to separate myself from society for a longer period of time to do so – even Thoreau's philosophy still affects the way I perceive nature. Although it is impossible for me to block out a week to spend in the woods in the near future, I have still realized that visiting the woods will bring me a sense of equanimity, at the very least. In times of stress, I will remember to return to my roots in nature, and it is impossible to say how those future experiences will affect my thinking.

"For the most part we allow only outlying and transient circumstances to make our occasions. They are, in fact, the cause of our distraction."

— "Solitude," page 4

IV – SLEEPY HOLLOW

For the sake of variety, I choose to visit Author's Ridge at Sleepy Hollow Cemetery for my final nature experience. Emerson's original concept for this cemetery was that it could double as a park for visitors to walk around, and the rolling hills preserve the feeling of a natural enclosure. As I climb up to the top of Author's Ridge, I realize that I always seem to be drawn to exploring hills, and that maybe I should branch out from this in the future.

As I climb up the hill, I quickly begin to recognize names on gravestones. I stop in front of the Hawthornes' family plot, trying to figure out which stone is Nathaniel's. "This is just his family," a woman says to her teenage son passing behind me. "Nathaniel Hawthorne is buried somewhere else. This is just his immediate family." Instinctively, I reach for my iPhone, aware that Google is the only resource in the world that can quickly confirm that Nathaniel Hawthorne is, in fact, buried in Sleepy Hollow Cemetery. It turns out I was right, but I also realize that I still have a lot of work to do to exemplify Thoreau's principle of simplification. Did this really matter enough to Google it? Thoreau would likely label this a petty concern, as "an honest man has hardly need to count more than his ten fingers, or in extreme cases he may add his ten toes, and lump the rest" ("Where I Lived..." 7).

I am still amazed by the number of American literary heroes who are buried on one hill. Thoreau's family sleeps across from the Hawthornes, the Alcotts rest slightly further down the path, and Emerson's rough boulder of a headstone is impossible to miss. In particular, I can understand why the transcendentalists would have enjoyed Concord, since the natural surroundings here easily encourage that type of deep thinking. Although Thoreau often dismisses the importance of outside influence, I think the community of writers that existed here would have inspired thinkers like him to develop their thoughts. Thoreau does mention that "certainly less frequency [in communication] would suffice for all important and hearty communications" ("Solitude" 5), so a lengthy solitary wandering might be Thoreau's interpretation of a sufficient break in socializing.

This type of community mentality might also have been what allowed the transcendentalists to become so forward-thinking in terms of individual thought. Although the transcendentalists were a group, they found kinship in their particular creative niche. In differentiating themselves from society, they found a collective voice. At the same time, they needed each other's influence in order to keep evolving. Thoreau may have overstated the value of solitude – what are thoughts when they are not shared with others? Even Thoreau published his philosophical conclusions. Isolation needs to be tempered by communication. When individual thinking comes to a standstill, other people help eliminate the roadblock.

I realize that this experience at Sleepy Hollow should be the end of my isolation with nature, at least for now. Maybe the opposite of Thoreau's ideas holds true: communing with nature needs to be punctuated by communing with other people. I cannot learn new things from nature if I have not attempted to apply what I have already learned to my own life. My time in nature allowed me to witness a stillness and tranquility that society could not grant me; now I must take this natural peace and discover how to incorporate it into my day-to-day existence. I will return to nature when I am searching for new answers.

Thoreau himself realized he needed to leave the woods when he understood he "had several more lives to live, and could not spare any more time for that one" ("Conclusion" 2). His experience had become a routine, and only a change of scenery could impel him to keep mentally developing. I come away from my Thoreau Challenge with a similar understanding, and I am willing to fully absorb my newfound knowledge before I return to nature once more.

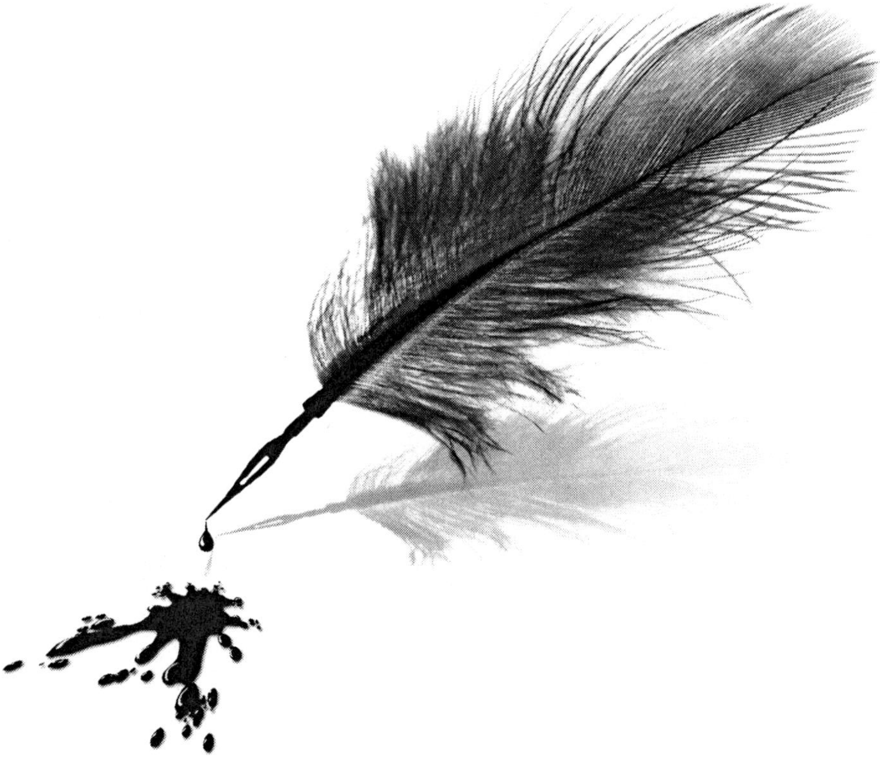

acknowledgements

I feel like I'm expected to make an Academy Awards acceptance speech in this section, though I lack sufficient experience in this area and may turn into a blubbering mess. Please redirect to YouTube so that Hugh Laurie can show you how it's done.

My friends and family are the most important piece of this puzzle, and without their support, I wouldn't be anywhere. Mom, Dad, Pop, Grandma, my Uncle Rob, and Chance – you're the most important people in my life, and also my greatest friends. Thank you for everything. Special thanks to my dad, the publishing wizard, without whom this book certainly would not have been possible.

Thanks to all of my English teachers and anyone who has ever critiqued my written work. Writing is a two-way street, and feedback is critical to anyone's growth as a writer. Each constructive comment has helped me arrive at this point, and I will never forget your crucial role in this process.

The staff of the CCHS Voice and my faculty advisor, Ms. Lee-DuBon, have played a vital role in my high school writing experience. Monday afternoons aren't complete without all of you!

Editor-in-chief Cheryl Lecesse has consistently supported me through the years, and I'm forever indebted to her for saving a few columns of *The Concord Journal* ink for me.

Without design guru Cindy Murphy's help, this book would be a formatting nightmare, edited in crayon, and stapled together. Thank you so much for saving the public from this fate.

Thanks too to Lauren Fleming and Elena Petricone for researching graphics and photos for this book, and to photographer Pierre Chiha for my official photo.

I'd also love to thank my college coach Marj Southworth for all her level-headed support and advice.

Thank you to Betsy Andersen for teaching me not only to play piano but also the value of kindness.

Finally, thank you, the reader, for making the decision to read this book! I can now comfortably assume that you have discerning taste in sophisticated literature.

about the author

Chloe Lizotte is a member of the Yale University class of 2016, and a 2012 graduate of Concord-Carlisle High School in Massachusetts where she served as editor-in-chief of the student newspaper *The Voice* and music director of radio station WIQH-FM.

Chloe has also authored a regular column about "historical eccentrics" for Concord's weekly newspaper *The Concord Journal* and in 2011 won the University of Virginia Book Award. Her twice-monthly radio show on WIQH won the station's "Outstanding Show of the Year" award three years running. She is an accomplished pianist and guitar player.

An avid snowboarder and runner, and a talented videographer, Chloe loves all things British (four trips to London) including attending a summer program at Cambridge College, England, in 2011. She has also visited Ireland, Scotland, Wales, Montreal and Paris. This is her first book.